COFFEE CULTURE

The Anthropology of Stuff is part of a new series, *The Routledge Series for Creative Teaching and Learning in Anthropology*, dedicated to innovative, unconventional ways to connect undergraduate students and their lived concerns about our social world to the power of social science ideas and evidence. Our goal is to help spark social science imaginations and, in doing so, new avenues for meaningful thought and action. Each "Stuff" title is a short text illuminating for students the network of people and activities that create their material world.

Coffee Culture: Local Experiences, Global Connections explores coffee as (1) a major commodity that shapes the lives of millions of people; (2) a product with a checkered and dramatic history; (3) a beverage with multiple meanings and uses (energizer, comfort food, addiction, flavoring, and confection); (4) an inspiration for humor and cultural critique; (5) an agricultural crop that can help protect biodiversity yet also threaten the environment; (6) a health risk and a health food; and (7) a focus for alternative trade efforts (fair trade and environmental certification programs). It presents coffee as a commodity that ties the world together, from the coffee producers and pickers who tend the plantations in tropical nations, to the middlemen and processors, to the consumers who drink coffee without ever having to think about how the drink reached their hands.

Catherine M. Tucker is a sociocultural and ecological anthropologist at Indiana University.

The Routledge Series for Creative Teaching and Learning in Anthropology
Editor: Richard H. Robbins, SUNY at Plattsburgh

This Series is dedicated to innovative, unconventional ways to connect under-graduate students and their lived concerns about our social world to the power of social science ideas and evidence. Our goal is to help spark social science imaginations and in doing so, new avenues for meaningful thought and action.

Available

Re-Imagining Milk by Andrea S. Wiley

Forthcoming

Lycra by Kaori O'Connor
Fake Stuff: China and the rise of Counterfeit Goods by Yi-Chieh Jessica Lin
Reading the iPod as an Anthropological Artifact by Lane DeNicola

COFFEE CULTURE

Local Experiences, Global Connections

Catherine M. Tucker

Routledge
Taylor & Francis Group

NEW YORK AND LONDON

First published 2011
by Routledge
711 Third Avenue, 8th Floor, New York, NY 10017

Simultaneously published in the UK
by Routledge
2 Park Square, Milton Park, Abingdon, Oxon OX14 4RN

Routledge is an imprint of the Taylor & Francis Group, an informa business

© 2011 Taylor & Francis

The right of Catherine M. Tucker to be identified as author of this work has been asserted by her in accordance with sections 77 and 78 of the Copyright, Designs and Patents Act 1988.

Typeset in Baskerville by Wearset Ltd, Boldon, Tyne and Wear

Library of Congress Cataloging-in-Publication Data
Tucker, Catherine M.
Coffee culture : local experiences, global connections / Catherine M. Tucker.
p. cm. – (Routledge series for creative teaching and learning in anthropology)
Includes bibliographical references and index.
1. Coffee–Social aspects. 2. Coffee–History. 3. Coffee–Health aspects. 4. Coffee industry–Social aspects.
I. Title.
GT2918.T83 2011
394.1'2–dc22   2010033196

ISBN13: 978-0-415-80024-2 (hbk)
ISBN13: 978-0-415-80025-9 (pbk)
ISBN13: 978-0-203-83124-3 (ebk)

To Percy and Alec

CONTENTS

ILLUSTRATIONS

Figures

Tables

SERIES FOREWORD

The premise of these short books on the *Anthropology of Stuff* is that stuff talks, that written into the biographies of everyday items of our lives—coffee, T-shirts, computers, iPods, flowers, drugs, and so forth—are the stories that make us who we are and that make the world the way it is. From their beginnings, each item bears the signature of the people who extracted, manufactured, picked, caught, assembled, packaged, delivered, purchased, and disposed of it. And in our modern market-driven societies, our lives are dominated by the pursuit of stuff.

Examining stuff is also an excellent way to teach and learn about what is exciting and insightful about anthropological and sociological ways of knowing. Students, as with virtually all of us, can relate to stuff, while at the same time discovering through these books that it can provide new and fascinating ways of looking at the world.

Stuff, or commodities and things, are central, of course, to all societies, to one extent or another. Whether it is yams, necklaces, horses, cattle, or shells, the acquisition, accumulation, and exchange of things is central to the identities and relationships that tie people together and drive their behavior. But never, before now, has the craving for stuff reached the level it has; and never before have so many people been trying to convince each other that acquiring more stuff is what they most want to do. As a consequence, the creation, consumption, and disposal of stuff now threaten the planet itself. Yet to stop or even slow down the manufacture and accumulation of stuff would threaten the viability of our economy, on which our society is built.

This raises various questions. For example, what impact does the compulsion to acquire stuff have on our economic, social, and political well-being, as well as on our environment? How do we come to believe that there are certain things that we must have? How do we come to value some commodities or form of commodities above others? How have we managed to create commodity chains that link peasant farmers in Colombia or gold miners in Angola to wealthy residents of New York or teenagers in Nebraska? Who comes up with the ideas for stuff and how do they translate those ideas into things for people to buy? Why do we sometimes consume stuff that is not very good for us? These short books examine such questions, and more.

Catherine M. Tucker's book *Coffee Culture: Local Experiences, Global Connections* beautifully captures the intent of the *Anthropology of Stuff* series. The book tells the story of coffee beginning with its role in establishing social meeting places in which scientists contemplated and discussed the nature of the universe, where political plots of various sorts were hatched, and where friends met to talk about their lives, experiences, and problems. She discusses the meaning that coffee has in people's lives, from its role as a marker of the daily work cycle to the meanings created by marketers to associate their product with desired moods and activities. And most of all, she describes the role of coffee as one of the world's most traded commodities, how it impacts workers occupying various points on the commodity chain, and how it affects the environments in which it is grown. She tells of the importance of coffee in the creation and maintenance of national identities and the impact it has on people's health. The story of coffee, as with much of the stuff of our lives, tells us about our culture and ourselves, and this book instructs us how to decipher that story.

PREFACE

Drinking coffee is the final step in a chain that connects us to farmers in tropical nations around the world who produce it. Through coffee, we are intimately tied to a global economic system that has evolved over half a millennium. Coffee is the second most valuable commodity traded on world markets, but it is produced by some of the world's poorest countries. Many of the 25 million farmers whose livelihoods depend on coffee earn barely a dollar a day. They live in some of the most biodiverse and endangered habitats of the world, and traditional coffee production has coexisted with forests by retaining shade and native trees. Yet market incentives favor sun-grown coffee, which requires forest clearing and use of toxic agrochemicals. Most recently, climate change processes appear to be threatening the future of coffee production as temperatures and rainfall become more variable. Thus coffee production has a bearing on some of the world's most pressing problems, including social inequality, biodiversity conservation, and environmental degradation.

For most of us, global issues of coffee production remain far from our consciousness. Instead, it is simply part of our lives. Even for those who avoid drinking it, coffee is inescapably present in Western society. For a beverage that has minimal nutritional value, it has acquired a plethora of meanings that vary across individuals and societies. Unlike most foods, coffee has raised an unending series of controversies over its possible impacts on health, social order, and individual well-being. More important for most of us is that coffee provides an excuse to hang out with friends, a vehicle for humorous social commentary, a way to relax, and a medium to promote productivity.

In this book I provide an overview of coffee, from its historical background and meanings and arguments over its use, to the pragmatic aspects of production and processing, to its entertaining dimensions. Through brief chapters focused on a central theme, I present coffee as a commodity that ties the world together, from the coffee producers and pickers who tend the plantations in tropical nations, to the middlemen and processors, to the consumers who drink coffee without ever having to think about how the drink reached their hands. I relate the material to theoretical insights from anthropology and the social sciences, which prove useful for interpreting the roles of coffee in our lives and the world.

I come to this book as someone whose perspectives on coffee have changed throughout my life. I did not drink coffee for the first 21 years of my life. A semester of study abroad in Colombia as a college student introduced me to coffee drinking and coffee plantations, but I did not find them as interesting as other aspects of Colombian culture. During graduate school I resorted to coffee as the cheapest and most pleasant way of keeping alert for long hours of study, and it became part of my daily routine. Not until starting my dissertation research, however, did I start to think about coffee seriously. I began studying community forest management in western Honduras in 1993, and since then have witnessed a dramatic transition from subsistence farming and traditional coffee production to export coffee production. Coffee became an obsession for me as I realized what it meant to the people who grew it, the ways that expanding plantations transformed people's relationships with each other and their natural environment, and the possibilities and problems that it posed. I confess fondness for coffee, the people who grow it, and the people who consume it, but I am appalled at the problems it creates and what I now know to be a history of agony hidden in each cup. I attempt to maintain intellectual objectivity, but my understanding is informed by affection and outrage, all for a deceivingly innocuous yet world-shaking substance that rests even now in a cup at my side.

ACKNOWLEDGMENTS

My odyssey of learning about coffee has involved countless hours talking with coffee producers and intermediaries, as well as representatives of governmental and non-governmental organizations who work with coffee production, marketing, and alternative trade approaches. I am grateful to all who gave of their time and insight. I am especially indebted to José María (Chema) Alberto, Erlindo Amaya, Leonardo Euseba, Jacquelyn García, Juan de la Cruz García, Justino García, Florentino Gómez, Mercedes Gómez, Elías Pérez, Joaquín Pérez, Uvence Menjívar, Mario Paz, Pedro Rivera, Gilbertina Romero, Enos Sánchez, Cristina Santos, Roberto Santos, and Julio Zelaya. I thank the members of the COCATECAL coffee cooperative, who have graciously shared their struggles, disappointments, and triumphs with me. Their creativity, determination, and courage inspire me. Eugenio Paz, Hermes Reyes, and Mario Ordoñez of the Honduran Coffee Institute (IHCAFE) have provided priceless assistance and information, along with knowledge from their decades of work with coffee producers and their own coffee plantations. Jessica Fonseca, Martha Moreno, Victor Moreno, Zoila Pérez, and Atanacio (Nacho) Pérez have given invaluable assistance with fieldwork over the years, but I am especially grateful for their friendship. Luisa García, Amadeo Santos, Carmen Rivera, Eladia Sánchez, Cupertino Sánchez, Desideria Pérez, Efrain Santos, and their families have welcomed me again and again into their homes, and I have learned a great deal over cups of coffee drunk together.

Teaching a course on coffee culture over the past four years has taught me even more about coffee—there's nothing like challenging questions from enthusiastic undergraduate and graduate students to compel a close examination of the facts and elicit new perspectives. Therefore I thank my students for pushing me to learn more, while also injecting their good humor and personal insights into my appreciation for coffee. Elise DeCamp deserves special acknowledgment for contributing her work on coffee humor, which she wrote originally as a research paper for the coffee culture class, and adapted for this book. I am grateful for her collaboration and upbeat disposition, which so well fit her research interests and promise as a scholar. I also thank LaDonna

BlueEye, who helped track down elusive facts, shared her expertise in public health, and compiled numerous documents on health, public policy, national laws, and alternative trade organizations related to coffee.

Any writing effort benefits from others' feedback and good editors. I am grateful for the suggestions of Warren Belasco of the University of Maryland, whose review comments helped me to improve the text. Special thanks go to Richard Robbins, who offered valuable suggestions and insights, and to Joanna Broderick, editor extraordinaire, who checked the entire manuscript carefully and assured consistency throughout. Any errors or oversights that remain are my own.

Most of all, I thank Percy and Alec for more than I can express, not least their good-natured tolerance (and liberal teasing) of my fascination with everything about coffee.

ACRONYMS AND ABBREVIATIONS

ADD   attention deficit disorder
ATO   Alternative Trade Organization
FLO   Fairtrade Labelling Organizations International
FNCC   National Federation of Coffee Growers of Columbia
FTF   Fair Trade Federation
ICA   International Coffee Agreement
ICO   International Coffee Organization
IFAT   International Fair Trade Association
ISI   import-substitution industrialization
ONCP   Overseas Needlepoint and Crafts Project
TMCM   Too Much Coffee Man, a character in a comic strip
TNC   transnational corporation
UNCTAD   United Nations Conference on Trade and Development
WFTO   World Fair Trade Organization

PART I

COFFEE CULTURE, SOCIAL LIFE, AND GLOBAL HISTORY

1

CULTURE, CAFFEINE, AND COFFEE SHOPS

The line at the coffee shop backs up to the door this weekday morning. Business-men, university students, and office workers wait patiently (or not) to place their orders. I am seated at one of the small tables, checking my email through the shop's free WiFi and drinking a delicious latté. Nearly all of the tables and easy chairs are occupied with individuals reading newspapers, couples talking, casually dressed young adults surfing the Internet with their laptops, and small groups of people who appear to be professionals on a coffee break. Conversations create a quiet back-ground murmur, and the shop maintains a comfortable ambience with stained wood décor, stylish wall art with a coffee theme, sofas and easy chairs around low coffee tables, and small circular tables with simple wooden chairs. Although a few customers choose tea, coffee is king here. Similar to most of the people in the shop, I want good, strong coffee in the morning. Anything else would be a poor substitute. I check my watch; it's time to get to the conference I am attending. I shut down my laptop, slip it into the case, and set my coffee mug on the counter. "Gracias," I say to the friendly barista. Walking out to the congested streets of Guatemala City, I realize that except for the language and a few other details, I might have been at a coffee shop in the USA or almost anywhere in the world.

Coffee shops have become a global phenomenon. Although coffee shops, or coffeehouses, have existed for nearly 500 years, in the past few decades they have experienced a dramatic expansion. It has become common to find coffee shops, coffee bars, and kiosks in places where they were once rare or non-existent—Hong Kong, Mexico City, Dublin, Rio de Janeiro, Tokyo, Sydney, New Delhi, or Johannesburg, and almost every major airport on the planet. Many factors contributed to the expansion, including the globalization of con-sumer culture, growing appreciation of high-quality coffee, and the public's eager acceptance of casual spots to study, relax, socialize, or pick up an ener-gizing drink. Growth of the World Wide Web played a role; it led to a synergis-tic convergence between caffeine and Internet access in coffeehouses and cyber cafés. In the USA, coffee shops are the fastest-growing segment of the restaurant business (Coffee Statistics Online 2010). Coffee shop expansion has been accompanied by gradual growth in global coffee consumption since 2000, after several decades of lagging consumption (ICO 2010; Reuters 2009). Coffee shops have become so ubiquitous that it is fair to say that they have impacted global culture (Clark 2007).

Growing coffee consumption and the popularity of coffee shops represent only the latest evidence of humanity's longstanding fondness for coffee drinking, which seems to have begun around the fifteenth century. During the sixteenth century, it spread throughout the Middle East and caught the attention of European travelers and traders. By the seventeenth century, coffee had become one of the first global commodities. Struggles to control its production and distribution led to wars, added fuel to Europe's colonial ambitions, exacerbated the eighteenth- and nineteenth-century slave trade, and set in motion economic and political relationships that still influence the global economy and international affairs (Bates 1997; Clarence-Smith and Topik 2003). Without coffee, the world as we know it would not exist.

Although rates of consumption fluctuate, coffee is a customary drink and an integral part of life in many societies. Worldwide, only non-commercial water, tea, and milk appear to be consumed more frequently than coffee, although ranks vary. Depending on the year, some sources rank coffee in second place after water, or carbonated beverages above coffee (Beverage Marketing Corporation 2009; Fletcher 2006; Justaboutcoffee.com 2007). Coffee's presence has become so integral to many people's lives that most continue to drink it even if prices rise or the economy slows. During the global economic recession of 2008, US coffee drinkers saved money by reducing visits to coffee shops and restaurants but increased the amount of coffee prepared at home. Expansion in specialty coffees continued unabated, driven by upper socioeconomic classes with disposable income (Mintel Oxygen 2009). Meanwhile, the amount of coffee consumed worldwide edged upward, with estimates exceeding 400 billion cups of coffee per year (Coffee Statistics Online 2010). The prevalence of coffee comes through in the media as well. Uncounted songs, comics, television shows, advertisements, and movies call attention to coffee and coffee shops, in minor or major ways. We receive news about possible health risks or benefits of drinking coffee, hear debates over the differences between fair trade and free trade coffee, and may read articles discussing the merits and problems of conventional vs. organic methods of production. Other beverages have their controversies, but none seem to be as protracted and recurrent as those surrounding coffee.

Why coffee? Why is it popular in the USA and nearly all the world? Why is it often a subject of controversies? Perhaps the more important question is why and how do coffee and its controversies matter for how we live our lives? In the coming pages, I consider these questions by looking at the culture, meanings, and histories of coffee, and how coffee production and consumption relate to some of the world's most pressing problems. The book is divided into four parts. The first part examines the whys of coffee, considering why (and how) coffee has acquired global presence and why it has become part of social life in the USA and around the world. It considers cultural experiences and meanings, theoretical approaches to understanding coffee, and the role of coffee in the development of the modern world system. The second part considers why and how coffee has been consistently subject to social commentary, critique, and controversy by looking at coffee humor, national identities, and medical debates. The third part explores the practical, social, economic, and environmental dimensions of coffee production. It asks the question: Can coffee production be environmentally and socially sustainable? In light of the uncertainties of coffee's sustainability, the fourth part ponders how international coffee markets and the global economic system have influenced the experiences of producers and consumers. It pays particular attention to the promise and pitfalls of fair trade coffee, and how consumer decisions, producer constraints, and the behavior of multinational corporations interplay to affect the potential for a global coffee system that is sustainable and fair. Exploring the many dimensions of coffee serves as a frame to consider how the world works today, experiences that we share, problems that challenge us, and struggles of people across time and space to assert their human rights (even the minor right to drink coffee) and build or maintain a society that works for them.

I begin by exploring why coffee is popular around the world. Caffeine, commonly recognized as the world's most popular drug, provides a launching point. Thereafter, I consider the role of culture in giving meanings to coffee, and then focus on the popularity and appeal of coffeehouses and cyber cafés. In subsequent chapters, I turn to the characteristics of coffee that have facilitated its global reach, the interpretations and expressions of coffee as a meaningful food, and the economic and historical developments that made coffee a preeminent beverage in the Western world.

Caffeine

The whys of coffee's popularity start with caffeine. After water and possibly milk, beverages that typically contain caffeine occupy the top spots in global beverage consumption: tea, coffee, and soft drinks. More than 60 plants produce caffeine naturally; the bitter alkaloid (a methylxanthine) repels many pests, bacteria, and fungi, and can limit weed growth (Lundsberg 1998; Prenosil *et al.* 1987). For humans, caffeine acts as a stimulant, but unlike many other drugs, caffeine is generally regarded as safe (Lamarine 1998). Caffeine-containing plants have been nurtured for their seeds, leaves, and nuts since early civilizations discovered their useful and pleasant qualities, which often included rich flavors linked to their caffeine content. Many of these plants also provide antioxidants and amino acids, which may enhance flavor and aroma while offering healthful benefits. One creative thinker theorized that plants produce caffeine as a ploy to enlist human assistance for reproductive success, hinting at the possibility of co-evolutionary processes between human society and the spread of caffeine-containing plants. Another author suggested facetiously that it is no coincidence that early humans evolved in Ethiopia, the birthplace of coffee (Wild 2004). From their earliest acknowledgment in the historical record, coffee beans were recognized for their medicinal and energizing effects. If people had not felt the effects of caffeine, it is unlikely that they would have been interested in collecting, processing, and preparing coffee beans.

Most sources of caffeine are consumed predominately at their place of origin. Popular sources of caffeine besides coffee beans are tea leaves, cacao (cocoa) beans, kola nuts, guarana seeds, and leaves of the yerba mate and qat trees. More tea is consumed in China and India than anywhere else, and those nations typically rank first and second in global tea production (Beverage Marketing Corporation 2009). The evergreen qat grows in the Middle East and eastern Africa, where people masticate the leaves; South Americans drink infusions of ground guarana seeds from the Amazon basin. Yerba mate tea is most popular in Uruguay, Paraguay, Brazil, and Argentina where the tree grows. Coffee and cacao (transformed into chocolate) break the pattern; the major consuming nations are located far from the sites where they grow. The same might have been true of tropical Africa's kola nuts, but most cola drinks today use synthetic flavors rather than kola nut extract (*Encyclopaedia Britannica* Online 2010).

Why is coffee enduringly and expansively popular, not simply where it grows, but in distant places? Caffeine content alone does not explain coffee's global popularity. While coffee can serve as a useful stimulant, a number of the world's coffee drinkers prefer decaffeinated coffees or prepare weak coffee to reduce caffeine content. Moreover, most locales have alternative or less expensive sources of caffeine available, including energy drinks, tea, chocolate, sodas, diet aids, analgesics, and caffeine tablets. Therefore coffee's popularity derives from more than its stimulating qualities; it encompasses social and cultural dimensions.

Coffee Culture

Coffee is a material substance, but culture infuses coffee with social and symbolic meanings. Culture can be defined as everything that humans think, have, and do as members of a society (Ferraro 2006). As water is for fish, culture is for humanity. It is our all-encompassing environment, and may be invisible unless we are separated from our own cultural contexts. Through culture, consuming coffee can affirm identity, express values, or affirm social ties. Coffee, as with many foods and beverages, has proven easily adaptable to different cultural contexts. Coffee combines well with many flavors and additives, therefore it fits within existing cuisines and evolving tastes (Coffee Statistics Online 2010). But what does "coffee culture" mean? As used here, it refers to the ideas, practices, technology, meanings, and associations regarding coffee. One could say that Starbucks has a specific coffee culture. Members express it by frequenting Starbucks cafés, knowing the terms to order specialty drinks (venti caramel macchiato, double tall low-fat soy decaf latté, no foam peppermint white chocolate mocha, and so forth), and perhaps supporting the ideals of Starbucks' mission statement or buying stock in the company. Coffee culture can unite actions, beliefs, and special knowledge to distinguish members from nonmembers, and the more knowledgeable from the less knowledgeable. Coffee has become popular as a local and global beverage in part because people see coffee as "our own." Coffee becomes meaningful for many reasons, which include the attachments or fondness that people develop for the ways that coffee is prepared and served, the places or contexts in which they consume coffee, and the ideas and feelings associated with drinking coffee. More of the world's coffee is consumed in homes than in any other place, thus coffee has become part of the comforts of family life for many adults. But coffee is also omnipresent in public life, where coffeehouses have played a key role in popularizing coffee and building coffee culture.

Coffeehouse Appeal

Coffee shops are as much about a place and an experience as they are about serving a beverage. Historically, coffeehouses gained fame as places for intellectual discussions, political debates, and free social expression (Connery 1997). Adam Smith wrote his influential political treatise *The Wealth of Nations* in a coffeehouse. Isaac Newton's ground-breaking *Principia Mathematica* grew out of a challenge to resolve an argument in a coffeehouse, during which no one had been able to prove why planets had elliptical orbits (Standage 2005). Today, coffee shops retain a reputation as social meeting places, but depending on their location and clientele, may also be places for study, relaxation, or simply to grab an invigorating drink. They appeal to the human desire for social interaction and connection to others, even if one plans to be alone. One Viennese commentator characterized coffeehouses as "the ideal place for people who want to be alone but need company for it" (Pendergrast 1999:380).

Through coffeehouses, people can sense or imagine the "small world" nature of society. Most of us have had moments of experiencing society as a small world, such as learning that someone we just met has a friend who grew up in our neighborhood. In "small world" theory, any pair of individuals in the world can be connected through only several degrees of separation (Milgram 1967). The game "six degrees of separation" plays on this idea. It is an open question of whether society is really a small world or humans try to envision small worlds as a way to make the world seem more comprehensible (Stafford 2003). In either case, coffeehouses provide opportunities to perceive a small world or create one, by offering something familiar in far-flung corners of the globe and our own hometowns.

While coffeehouses share common aspects—especially coffee and sociality—they vary in the customers they attract through unique atmospheres, a variety of services and ancillary products (books, music, art work), and different qualities, origins, blends, or preparations of coffee. These distinctions have been accentuated through intentional—and sometime accidental—niche marketing, which had antecedents in seventeenth-century London, where coffeehouses catered to different clienteles and professions. Niche marketing in coffee shops took off in the USA during the 1980s in response to changes in coffee-drinking patterns. Between 1960 and 1988, the percentage of coffee drinkers in the USA fell gradually from 74 percent to 50 percent (Roseberry 1996). Small coffee roasters and independent coffee vendors realized that they needed to expand their clientele, and attract young people who had grown up preferring soft drinks. Meanwhile, the transnational corporations (TNCs) that dominated coffee markets (e.g., Nestlé, General Foods, Philip Morris) sought to increase their profits and decided to produce successively cheaper (and therefore less flavorful) coffee, which most likely contributed to falling demand. Independent entrepreneurs took advantage of the lack of good coffee to draw clients who appreciated quality, flavor, and variety (Roseberry 1996).

Starbucks became an early trendsetter by introducing the modern coffeehouse to US society (Dicum and Luttinger 1999). It started small, but distinguished itself by a commitment to quality and as "a third place" apart from work and home; by 2009 it had 16,706 stores in over 50 countries (Starbucks 2010a, 2010b). As Starbucks grew into a global coffee behemoth, it gained a great deal of attention, and inspired a generation of coffee entrepreneurs to open their own coffee shops. Starbucks gained a reputation for purposefully driving local coffee shops and smaller chains out of business (Clark 2007). Many independent coffeehouses, however, have competed successfully through excellent attention to faithful customers, and providing unique beverages, atmospheres, or services to complement local tastes or attract certain groups. In Banda Aceh, Indonesia, customers like coffee poured over a raw egg to drink for breakfast (Iijima 2010). A Taiwanese coffee chain serves a hugely popular coffee topped with salt-infused foam (Greenberg 2010). In Houston, Coffeegroundz Café expanded its clientele by taking to-go orders through Twitter (O'Grady 2008). Creative niche marketing has helped independent operations to survive; they account for more than half of the coffeehouses in the USA (*Tea & Coffee* 2004).

Cyber Cafés Linking Physical and Virtual Coffeehouses

By providing Internet access, cyber cafés opened new horizons for coffeehouse customers to experience "small worlds." While traveling, I've come to rely on coffeehouses as places that offer free or low-cost Internet access. The advent of Skype and international web-based phone calling augmented the attraction of cyber cafés, especially in places where the average person cannot afford Internet fees or long-distance telephone service. Not long ago, I received a call from a Honduran friend who lives in a village without electricity or phone service. My friend explained that he was calling from a new cyber café in the district capital, at the cost of only a few cents. I still recall the delight at being in touch, and realizing that we could now communicate more easily. The Internet allows coffeehouses to extend their reach as places of social inter-action and centers to exchange news and information. The interactions may be virtual, but coffeehouses provide a physical bridge for communicating through cyberspace. One industry report noted, "People are now given the option to make a connection over a cup of coffee and/or over the internet" (Holmes 2004:3). The Internet operates with the social dynamism, challenges to the status quo, and disdain for authority that once characterized Europe's early coffeehouses; thus the Internet acts as a virtual coffeehouse (Connery 1997). It seems logical that brick-and-mortar coffeehouses embraced the Internet as an extension of their role as places for social interaction.

Local and Global Dimensions in Coffeehouses

Coffeehouses can recreate and symbolize the global influence of Western coffee culture while expressing the uniqueness of a specific locale or cultural context. The coffee shop I patronized in Guatemala City created an atmosphere reminiscent of a Starbucks, but used ceramic mugs more than paper cups, and featured photos with scenes of rural Guatemala and Mayan peoples in coffee fields. The combination acknowledged global coffee culture and Guatemalan coffee traditions at once. Through history and across cultures, however, coffee has meant more than the sociality and casual community of coffeehouses. Coffee has been associated with subjugation, revolution, resistance, and intense debates (Chapter 7), but also family life and friendship. Drinking coffee has taken on meanings and values that fit specific locales, while resonating broadly with globalized understandings. The modern world presents many interstices where local experiences and understandings interact with globally disseminated messages and representations. Anthropologists and food scholars wrestle with interpreting this complex landscape of meaning and practice through theoretical approaches that address the whys and hows of foods as meaningful substances, to which we now turn.

Questions for Reading, Reflection, and Debate

1. Why do you think coffeehouses are popular?
2. What is niche marketing? How does it relate to the concept of "coffee culture"?
3. Consider the "small world" theory. What experiences in your life would support the theory? What experiences would seem to contradict it?

2

THEORIES OF FOOD AND SOCIAL MEANINGS OF COFFEE

Food is always about more than simply what fills the stomach.

(Rouse and Hopkins 2004:226)

What is the most valuable commodity traded on world markets? If you're thinking petroleum, you're right. But did you know that coffee is the second most valuable commodity in the world? Think about that for a second. The most valuable commodity serves as the planet's premier fuel source. Moreover, petroleum and its derivatives find their way into innumerable goods in all facets of our lives—plastics, electronics, carpets, building materials, clothing, furniture, machinery, pesticides, and many chemical products. By contrast, what does coffee provide? Coffee offers little nutritional benefit, and it is not a major component in any product other than itself. From an objective perspective, coffee is not necessary or integral for social or individual well-being, although coffee fanatics probably would disagree. Nevertheless, coffee generates more trade dollars than any other food, manufactured good, or natural resource besides petroleum. The only exception occurs when coffee prices collapse and other goods temporarily exceed coffee's global trade value. Pundits point out that petroleum fuels industry and transportation, while coffee fuels labor productivity. In this rather facetious view, petroleum and coffee rank first and second in global trade because they are complementary energy sources. But why is coffee more important economically than other sources of caffeine? The first chapter proposed that coffee's popularity relates to its combination of social utility and cultural associations, as illustrated with the example of coffeehouses, which help to meet human needs for social interaction and a sense of community. In theory, teahouses could offer the same things, but it seems strange to suppose that we could be flocking to Starbucks tea shops.

What explains differing perceptions of coffee, tea, and other beverages? What are the reasons for a group of people to prefer one food over another, or deem certain foods as especially desirable while other foods seem ordinary?

How do foods acquire meanings, and how do meanings and attitudes toward food interrelate with other aspects of social life? What roles does food play in a globalizing world? These are the kinds of questions that social theorists and food scholars have been exploring. Since the 1950s, food has become an increasingly pertinent topic for scholars studying cultural identity, social change, and globalization (Mintz and Du Bois 2002). Coffee offers interesting opportunities for study because of its ubiquitous presence in modern social life, its relationships to global markets as well as group and national identities, and its economic and political dimensions.

A number of approaches exist for theorizing about the relationships among food, culture, meaning, and social change. I introduce three theoretical approaches that help us think about the role of coffee, its meanings, and its popularity around the world. The first approach, presented by Claude Lévi-Strauss (1983, 2008), proposes that societies follow similar patterns for interpreting foods due to the way the human mind works. By understanding the mental structures that underlie perceptions, we gain insight into how societies assign values and meanings to food. The second approach, developed by Pierre Bourdieu (1984), examines taste in food and other cultural preferences as emerging from social-class differences, and the tensions and contrasts among groups in complex societies. The third approach investigates the connections within and across societies to understand the uses, ideas, and meanings of food, and explores the economics of global trade. It asks how these connections shape our lives, and what the implications are for the environment, local and global society, and the ongoing evolution of the modern world system. Each of these approaches contributes to interpreting coffee's role in modern society.

Raw, Cooked, or Rotten? Mental Structures and Perceptions of Food, Nature, and Culture

Cross-cultural commonalities in meanings and values ascribed to foods may relate to ways that the human mind interprets and categorizes the world. Lévi-Strauss (1983, 2008), a renowned French anthropologist, proposed that foods fall into one of three broad categories: "raw," "cooked," or "rotted." After collecting information on myths and food beliefs around the world, he argued that while societies vary in how they interpret the meanings of food, they still deal with dualities such as raw/cooked, raw/rotted, and cooked/rotted, which symbolize and echo other oppositions: nature/culture, good/bad, edible/inedible, self/other, desirable/repulsive. Raw foods are "natural," "unprocessed," and "wild"; they often require some kind of preparation, such as washing, peeling, and cutting to be deemed edible. Cooked foods have been transformed through roasting, boiling, or smoking to become "civilized." Societies tend to regard roasting, boiling, or smoking as having different levels of prestige.

Among Western societies, roasting tends to have higher prestige than boiling. The relative status of these forms of cooking varies across history and people. There is no universal way to ascertain a food's position in a cultural system of meaningful oppositions and dualities. Instead, it is necessary to understand a people's perspectives and experiences.

The way society categorizes a food reflects its prestige, usefulness, and potential risks, which relate to historical, political, and economic processes, and preferences whose roots may be long forgotten. Perceptions of food risks emerge because of the ways that society links edible substances to social values and experiences. Edible food discarded by restaurants and grocery stores becomes "rotted" the moment it hits the dumpster (even if a hungry person retrieves that food to eat, he or she would be aware of how society classifies the food). In the USA, insects are considered to be inedible, but in most of the world, people recognize certain insects as delicious and nourishing foods (Bryant *et al.* 2003). The television show *Fear Factor* played upon Western distastes by challenging contestants to do potentially unpleasant things, such as eating insects, while competing for monetary prizes. Contestants who chose to eat the insects symbolically and physically transformed the inedible to the edible, defying one social norm in order to fulfill another social norm: willingness to sacrifice for monetary gain. In forcing contestants to choose between social norms, the show compelled the audience to question where their preferences and priorities lay. Can something repulsive be made tolerable by the possibility of enrichment (and fleeting fame)? Few Westerners found the answers simple. Lévi-Strauss's perspective (1983, 2008) helps us to understand that the dilemma emerges from Western perceptions of underlying oppositions. For someone from an insect-eating society, there would be no opposition or repulsion, and no dilemma.

Coffee does not present moral conundrums for most drinkers, but how does society interpret coffee? Clearly, coffee is "cooked." It has been roasted, ground, and mixed with water by some means—boiling, percolating, filtering, pressing, or steaming under pressure. In this sense, coffee is a complex culinary creation that signifies civilized society. Yet coffee is also represented as something "natural," "wild," and uncivilized in Western cultures, because of its associations with exotic origins and dangerous diseases that medical science does not understand well. The perceived risks of coffee led certain religions to ban it and some physicians to warn against it, while the perceived benefits and status of coffee resulted in the creation of coffee breaks and contributed to its prevalence in social life.

Society, Class, and Taste

The meanings and use of coffee may also be influenced by social relations and class divisions. The French social scientist, Pierre Bourdieu (1984), conducted a detailed survey of the French population to explore relationships among education, occupation, cultural knowledge, economic resources, preferences, and behaviors. The analysis found that different occupational classes in French society express distinctive patterns in cultural knowledge, economic resources and preferences, and taste. Members of privileged classes, composed of those with well-paying jobs and/or inherited wealth, have tastes in food, art, music, clothing, and so on that relate to greater economic resources and higher education in prestigious schools. They have autonomy to make choices, and can define luxury. Among the intermediate and less-privileged classes, the levels of education and economic resources restrict options, and necessity influences their choices. They develop meaningful preferences for food among the options available to them. Bourdieu's work, which cannot be treated adequately here, showed that the conditions of people's lives shape how they structure, perceive, and experience the world, and therefore evolve distinctive lifestyles and ways of thinking. Class differences thus entail much more than economic inequality. They encompass contrasting knowledge, perceptions, and preferences. These differences inform and justify symbolic, political, and material struggles between classes within a society. Bourdieu's insights suggest that meanings and preferences associated with coffee, as well as knowledge and access to information about coffee, likely will vary across different social classes in any given society. Moreover, ideas and meanings are subject to negotiation and contestations as different classes in society interact and attempt to advance their interests and values.

Complex Connectivity: Food Production, Consumption, and Globalization

Tracing the connections that constitute global networks can reveal relationships and processes that have shaped the implications and meanings of particular foods. A number of studies have examined the histories, social-environmental interconnections, and commodity chains of specific foods. They have discovered unexpected relationships and impacts that have helped to create the modern world (Cohen 1997; Kurlansky 1997; Ryan and Durning 1997; Zuckerman 1998). Mintz's work *Sweetness and Power* (1986) explored the evolution of sugar from a rare spice to an integral component of European diets. He showed how a single commodity linked Europe, Africa, and the Americas in patterned exchanges of goods and humanity (slave trade). Sugar production and consumption played critical roles in the Industrial Revolution, and had ramifications for society, ethnic and political relations, and worker health. Foster's study of Coca-Cola (Foster 2008) explored the complications and contradictions of globalization, as consumers around the world become tied into world markets. He points out that commodities can disembed social relationships and undermine cultures, or be re-embedded in local relations and contexts in ways that challenge or mock globally disseminated meanings and values. For example, women in Papua New Guinea began to use empty soda cans to carry and cook a meal of rice when they visited friends; the cans filled a social need once met by bamboo tubes. Thus local people can creatively integrate the global into the local (Foster 2008:11).

Coffee, similar to many other foods and commodities, is caught up in global networks that connect people who live in vastly different cultural, environmental, and economic contexts. Global networks create relationships across great distances, between producers and consumers, among consumers with shared concerns, and across divides of culture and perceptions. Enjoying a cappuccino, eating mocha ice cream, or smelling the aroma of fresh-brewed coffee only occurs because distant parts of the world are tied together in a global chain of people who grow, pick, transport, process, distribute, and finally consume coffee beans. Over the last century, the coffee chain has experienced globalizing processes, which can be understood as complex connectivity associated with intensifying connections and interdependencies (Tomlinson 1999). These evolving relationships have led to novel alliances and consumer–producer linkages, as in the fair trade movement. Global networks provide contexts in which struggles occur over flows of money and the distribution of costs and benefits from trade, as well as meanings and values.

Examining the economic and political relations that structure the global coffee system, and the vast numbers of people involved in coffee production and consumption, helps to explain why coffee is an extraordinarily valuable and contested commodity. An estimated 25 million farmers grow coffee across 60 countries. Another 100 million people depend on coffee for their livelihoods as coffee pickers, middlemen, processors, roasters, transporters, and distributors (Consumers International 2005; Osorio 2002). That number doesn't count the factory owners and workers who produce the chemical inputs that growers often use to increase their yields, or the laborers who manufacture the equipment used to process or transport the coffee. All of these people work to supply enough coffee to meet global demand. Tens of millions of people—over 100 million people in the USA alone—drink coffee. But only four major TNCs—Nestlé, Sara Lee, Kraft Foods, and Tchibo—dominate the coffee market and hold major brands. Together, they purchase 60 percent of the world's green (unroasted) coffee beans (Future Trends 2001) and have the power to constrain prices paid to producers, while maintaining prices of coffee sold to consumers.

Theoretical Integration for Examining Coffee Meanings and Values

Each of these theoretical approaches helps to interpret the meanings and popularity of coffee in modern society, and how they vary across classes.

Consider espresso drinks, which appear to carry the highest social prestige among various ways to prepare coffee. It requires special machinery and training to create a perfect shot of espresso, a fine latte, or a cappuccino. Lévi-Strauss (1983) would not be surprised. He pointed out that different social meanings map consistently to different types of food preparation: the high-prestige activities involve greater patience, more complex technology and resources, or greater skill to carry out well, which is true of espresso. Following Bourdieu (1984), we would expect that people who drink the higher-prestige and more expensive coffee are more likely to be people from privileged social classes. Research surveys indeed reveal that consumers with higher incomes drink specialty coffees more frequently than lower-income consumers. People who prefer espresso drinks may also be perceived as more ambitious or wealthy than those who drink regular coffee. Thus coffee can be a marker of socioeconomic class in that people from other classes may identify espresso with a higher class, and members of higher classes can choose to reaffirm their social class by conforming to preferences for specialty coffees. It would be difficult for working-class coffee drinkers to spend the extra money to buy specialty coffee on a regular basis, and if they have never been exposed to the information that bird-friendly coffee supports biodiversity conservation, for example, how will they evaluate or justify the higher cost of the coffee? Indeed, a regular coffee blend of a major label, such as Folgers or Maxwell House, may be preferred because it is familiar, reliable, reasonably priced for the household budget, and probably preferred among friends and associates.

Yet a shot of espresso or a cappuccino is within the economic grasp of the general population, at least as a special treat. People who are not members of the more privileged classes may choose to consume these drinks not only out of enjoyment, but also to appear affluent, discriminating, or tasteful. They can, for a brief period, indulge themselves in an experience associated with wealth. Similarly, people of wealth may choose regular, filtered coffee to signal humility, lack of pretension, modest origins, or genuine class-inspired preferences that eschew the indulgences of espresso. The choice of coffee can thus signal membership in or identification with a social class, but it can also be used to transcend, contradict, or undermine social-class divisions. The malleability of coffee to send many messages is part of what makes it appealing to people of many social backgrounds.

Similarly, theoretical examinations of connectivity help to illuminate the emergence of fair trade coffee. In recent decades, the experiences of coffee producers have been disseminated through films (e.g., *Black Gold*), news releases, and scholarly publications. The information, itself a product of global connections, has encouraged people to consider where coffee comes from, how it reaches our cups, and the environmental and social consequences of commodity chains. It was through awareness of the difficult situations faced by coffee farmers that consumers in Europe and the USA developed fair trade coffee. The obscure connections between northern consumers and tropical producers became more apparent with the development of fair trade as an alternative to the standard commodity chain. Producers' perceptions of their ties to consumers also became clearer, and many participate in fair trade and environmental certifications to meet what they perceive as consumer preferences. Yet both sides face challenges from TNCs, and have experienced disappointments and difficulties in their distanced relationships with each other and the global coffee market system.

Considering theoretical approaches to food reveals that each one helps to understand certain aspects of coffee. No single theory explains all of coffee's multifaceted meanings, values, and purposes in social life and global relationships. While these theories help us to understand the contexts in which social meanings and values emerge, we still fall short of answering why coffee is one of the world's most valuable and popular commodities. It is worth considering the role of the USA and its relationship with coffee.

Questions for Reading, Reflection, and Debate

1. What foods do you consider to be high prestige? Low prestige? Why? How do the theories of Lévi-Strauss and Bourdieu prove helpful (or not) for classifying foods?
2. In what ways might Lévi-Strauss's classification system be problematic? What foods might be hard to fit within the classification system of raw, cooked, or rotten?
3. What is the most disgusting thing that you have ever been given to eat? What did you do? Why?
4. What foods do you prefer? In what ways do your preferences differ from your friends or other students? Explain whether these differences relate to your socioeconomic background or other factors.
5. How do your favorite or frequently consumed foods depend on global connections and commodity chains?

3

COFFEE CULTURE, HISTORY, AND MEDIA IN COCA-COLA LAND

It's 8:35 a.m. this Monday morning, and the line at the Starbucks across from the Indiana University campus spills onto the sidewalk. Walking by, I estimate that at least 20 people are waiting for their coffee, nearly all of them professors, students, or administrative staff. I decide to go to the next nearest coffee shop, only one block away. But the line at that shop is at least as long; it draws even more people than Starbucks due to its fresh-baked muffins and bagels. I don't have time to wait in a long line, and if I don't get my coffee soon, I'll have to run to my first meeting without it. I hate the thought of starting my day without coffee. But I have the choice of three other independent coffee shops and Dunkin' Donuts within a one-block radius. Which one, I wonder, will be least likely to have a line? The answer comes to me—I'll go to Soma, the only coffee shop with a line of self-serve Thermoses, filled every 15 minutes with fresh-brewed, fair trade coffee. Even if there's a line, it won't take long. I go by a delicatessen on my way; it's crowded with people eating breakfast and drinking coffee from mugs. Practically jogging now, I cross the street, turn the corner, and duck into Soma. The line moves quickly; in less than seven minutes I have paid for my coffee and filled my cup. On the way to the meeting, I pass the Dunkin' Donuts and another line of people wanting coffee. I may be a few minutes late for my 9 a.m. meeting. That's okay; I have my coffee, and a few others may be late for the same reason. Going by the number of busy coffee shops, someone might think that the campus runs on coffee. Maybe it's true.

Like most other adults in the USA, I drink coffee. We are the reason that the USA is the world's largest coffee consumer, representing about 20 percent of the world's total coffee intake. We are a nation of caffeine, fast food, coffee shops, and life lived too often at an unrelenting 24-hour-a-day pace. Recent research finds that 82 percent of the USA's adult population drinks coffee, and 48 percent drink it daily (*Tea & Coffee* 2007). On average, US coffee drinkers consume about three cups of coffee a day (1.6 cups per capita). We don't come close to the Finns, who are the world's most avid coffee drinkers, consuming from four to ten cups daily (Coffee Research Institute 2006; Tufts University 2008). But Finland represents a small proportion of the world's population, and the USA is the world's third most populous country. Moreover, the USA has the world's highest Gross Domestic Product, and it is a global trade giant. The question "Why is coffee one of the world's most popular beverages?" needs to acknowledge simple demographic and economic realities: the USA's combination of wealth, trading power, and fondness for coffee have made an important contribution to coffee's global importance. But the story isn't that straightforward. The USA is one of the world's largest consumers of all beverages (Food&Drinkeurope.com 2003). Coffee competes for consumer preference against tea, carbonated soft drinks, energy drinks, and a smorgasbord of health drinks, juices, milk, and bottled water, not to mention beer, wine, and spirits. Why then did coffee become important in the USA? And how has it retained its position in a highly competitive beverage market?

A Brief History of Coffee in the USA

Coffee consumption in the USA stretches back to the seventeenth century, but the emergence of the coffee habit and its integration into daily life occurred gradually. In the colonial period, tea was at least as popular as coffee. American preference for coffee over tea emerged through specific historical events leading up to the Revolutionary War (Chapter 7) but it endures because social values and national identity became linked to coffee drinking. In 1830, per capita coffee consumption stood at three pounds per year, and it was associated with society's elite (Roseberry 1996). In the next 100 years, global production expanded, prices dropped, and roasting technology improved greatly. The drip filter-brewing method was invented in 1908 by a German housewife, Frau Melitta Benz. The method spread rapidly to the Americas where it became more popular than the traditional method of boiling coffee, which tends to result in a bitter taste (Weinberg and Bealer 2002). Through the mid nineteenth century, farmers and workers became coffee drinkers. By 1930, coffee drinking had spread throughout society, and annual coffee consumption had increased to around ten pounds per capita. This transition took place in association with the expansion of industrial production and a determined promotional effort by the US coffee lobby. In 1921, the Joint Coffee Publicity Committee conducted an ad campaign that advised customers to drink coffee to restore energy when they felt tired in late morning or late afternoon. The coffee lobby financed studies on coffee's effects on alertness, and distributed results showing that coffee consumption helped to maintain productivity. That same initiative helped businesses set up coffee stations, and coffee breaks became part of the work day (Jiménez 1995a). The coffee lobby also promoted the integration of coffee drinking into everyday home life through a home economics service, which advised housewives on how to prepare coffee to keep their husbands happy. In the same interval, instant coffee became available, and new forms of coffee consumption such as iced and flavored concoctions emerged.

Coffee in Daily American Life

By the middle of the twentieth century, coffee had deep cultural and historical roots in American society, and was part of American enculturation. From a young age, most children observe adults drinking coffee, or see it being served at public events. Curious children may beg to sample it, because American society believes that coffee is for adults (unlike a number of other societies, which offer coffee to children). Coffee is omnipresent in daily life. At breakfast time, waitresses serve coffee as they hand out menus. Nearly all business offices have coffee pots to serve clients and provide for employees. Students studying for tests and people working night shifts or facing deadlines turn to coffee and other caffeinated beverages to stay awake. Sitting on a table, accompanied by a bowl of sugar and powdered creamer or a pitcher of milk, the coffee pot occupies a prominent location at club meetings, church potlucks, banquets, weddings, funerals, and special events. For millions of people, drinking coffee is part of their morning ritual. Even if we do not drink coffee, most of us accept that coffee can help us stay awake, has a place in many social activities, and gives off an aromatic invitation to drink it.

Coffee in the Media: Ads, Slogans, and Social Values

As indicated, the media has played a role in shaping coffee consumption and perceptions of coffee. From the dissemination of medical studies of coffee to advertisements and slogans designed by industrial psychologists and marketing experts, consumers encounter information and representations of coffee that are often aimed to invoke a reaction: to drink a certain brand, or to consume more (or less) coffee. At the same time, consumers have been active agents by embracing or resisting media promotions, and at times pressuring companies to make changes in their products through open dislike or opposition (New Coke comes to mind), or ignoring a product.

Ad campaigns can draw on social values and established preferences to try to sell goods by association. Examples of ad campaigns for Colombian coffee, Taster's Choice/Nescafé Gold Blend (depending on the market), and Folgers illustrate some of the approaches intended to gain loyal customers and a broader market share. Colombia has long enjoyed a reputation as a producer of fine coffee. Its fame was so early and prominent that its coffee gave the name "Columbian Milds" to an entire category of coffee traded on international markets. The nation has struggled, however, to maintain its market share in the face of competition from quality niche coffees, and abundant, cheaper coffees from Brazil, Vietnam, and East Africa. During the 1990s, the Colombian coffee lobby designed a new ad campaign to disseminate the slogan "Grab Life by the Beans." Playing off a well-known American slang phrase, the Colombian ads featured athletes risking their lives as they skied off glaciers, surfed through monster waves, and climbed mountain peaks. The ads aimed explicitly to attract young adults to drink more coffee, because coffee consumption had slumped in the 18–30 age group as caffeinated soft drinks gained popularity. The ads received favorable attention, but it is not clear how much difference the ads made in encouraging more people to try Colombian coffee.

A similar situation occurred for the instant coffee Nescafé Gold Blend/Taster's Choice in a highly successful television promotion. It played upon American fascination with romance, and tried to attract young coffee drinkers by presenting the instant coffee as rich-tasting, convenient, and sensual (Reichert 2003). A series of ads featured an attractive young woman and her equally attractive male neighbor, who gradually fell in love over successive, shared cups of the instant coffee (the male protagonist, Anthony Stewart Head, is now known for his role in *Buffy the Vampire Slayer*). Although the ads achieved high recognition (perhaps the only ad campaign to rival serial soap operas), the company discovered that audiences cared more about watching the ads than increasing their consumption of Nescafé/Taster's Choice. Despite this and other efforts, instant coffees have yet to attain a reputation for matching the flavor of freshly brewed coffee.

Folgers became a successful brand by promoting its coffee as "Mountain Grown," and staking a claim to high quality. Through the 1960s and 1970s, a series of television ads presented Folgers as the answer to housewives' coffee-brewing shortcomings, and a way to encourage a happier married life. More recently, ads show Folgers coffee as an integral part of family life and fun social happenings. The company also promotes a variety of coffee types to appeal to a broad clientele. Maxwell House gained earlier and enduring recognition by wisely embracing the coffee slogan "Good to the last drop" in 1917. The phrase had been coined by President Theodore Roosevelt upon finishing a cup of coffee prepared by the Maxwell House Hotel of Nashville, Kentucky (Beyer 2007). It became one of the most famous and enduring slogans in US marketing. To this day, Folgers, Maxwell House, Taster's Choice, and various labels carrying the specification "Colombian coffee" can be found in grocery store coffee aisles.

During the late nineteenth century, soda waters became popular beverages throughout the USA. Soda fountains prepared dozens or hundreds of flavored beverages, many of which carried health claims, and were generally confined to local markets (Pendergrast 2000). In some ways, soda fountains of the late nineteenth and early twentieth centuries were precursors to late-twentieth-century coffee shops as gathering places, but they never gained a global trajectory. Sodas presented a contrasting option to coffee, although coffee retained its predominance as a morning drink and for coffee breaks. Both beverages were inexpensive and available to all social classes.

In the 1960s, coffee consumption began a gradual decline. Coffee companies' ads promoted the quality and social relevance of their brands, but customers had begun to drift to alternative drinks. At this time, the major brand companies (Folgers, Maxwell House, Hills Brothers) and a few regional companies dominated coffee sales. Coffee had become a standardized product, and the average consumer couldn't taste any difference between the brands. In this context, companies began substituting arabica coffees with cheaper, bitter robusta coffee, at the cost of flavor and aroma (Roseberry 1996). They advertised the idea of quality, while gradually replacing high-quality beans with cheaper beans, believing that consumers would not notice the difference. As one scholar notes, they had begun a race to sell the cheapest coffee possible, while maintaining prices (Clark 2007). After all, they had very little competition. They left the door open for the independent roasters who had not been swallowed up and who, in the 1970s, started experimenting with quality beans, creating their own blends and selling fresh-roasted coffees. One of these small roasters opened in 1971 at Pike Place Market in Seattle under the name of Starbucks. It developed a faithful clientele, but remained a roasting shop until an ambitious entrepreneur, Howard Schultz, bought it in 1987 and dared to open a coffee shop (Starbucks Coffee Company 2010b). By that time, soft drinks had become the dominant beverage in the USA, and Coca-Cola had become a global symbol of American culture.

Coca-Cola vs. Coffee

Soft drinks have been competing with coffee as sources of caffeine for over a century. In some ways soft drinks and coffee seem to be very different drinks. Soft drinks are sweet, bubbly, and best when served cold. Although Coca-Cola and many other sodas began as putatively healthful combinations of herbal and other natural extracts, most soft drinks today are artificially flavored. Coffee remains a natural product. It can be served hot or cold (would anyone drink Coca-Cola as a steaming hot beverage?) and prepared to fit individual preferences with or without sugar, milk, or other flavorings. By contrast, soft drinks are usually consumed without additives. Coca-Cola does not stand for much adulteration, aside from Coke floats and a few flavored versions (e.g., Cherry Coke). But coffee, Coca-Cola, and other caffeinated beverages have played off of the effects of caffeine as invigorating and uplifting.

Over the course of the twentieth century, coffee and soft drinks (especially Coca-Cola) have fought to gain or maintain popularity with American consumers. In the process, soft drinks became the largest category of beverage consumed in the USA. Soft drinks as well as coffee transformed as consumer tastes evolved and markets became more global. The growth of Starbucks and purveyors of specialty coffees have "decommoditized" coffee; it is no longer a single, identifiable good but many unique goods, which may take on different meanings and associations. Consumers have lessened reliance on major coffee brands in a widely and wildly diversified market. While Coca-Cola has diversified by adding other beverages to its product line, it has defended vigorously the integrity of its name and reputation, and prosecuted any attempt to infringe upon it. Although Starbucks defends its name, it is known for coffee shops more than as a brand of coffee.

In 2006, Coca-Cola attempted to appropriate part of the coffee market by introducing Coca-Cola Blāk, a coffee-flavored Coca-Cola beverage. Introduced first in France (Wentz and Mussey 2006), the 2007 attempt to introduce it in the USA proved a fiasco. When journalist Anderson Cooper tasted it on a national TV broadcast, he spat it out. (YouTube has clips of people praising or vilifying the beverage). Coca-Cola announced that it would discontinue the product in August 2007 (Stanford 2007). Evidently, coffee-flavored Coke could not replace the real thing.

Undeniably the preeminent American soft drink, Coca-Cola became a national and global success through a combination of strategic marketing, wise (and not so wise) business decisions, and luck. It has been called the most recognizable American product in the world, reaching more countries than the United Nations (Pendergrast 2000). Coca-Cola originated in the USA and, therefore, could represent itself as something uniquely and especially American, which is something that coffee cannot claim. Invented by John Pemberton in 1886, and acquired by Asa Candler through dubious means, Coca-Cola spread through aggressive and clever advertising. Early on, Coca-Cola presented itself as eminently American and democratic in its availability to all classes. The company has repeatedly identified itself with "The American Way of Life" (Weiner 2002). "Coke is the Real Thing" implied not only the authenticity of the product but American values of honesty, openness, and good value, while defying the possibility that any competitor could measure up (as Pepsi gained market share).

When the USA entered World War II, Coca Cola arranged with the US military to develop bottling centers and supply lines wherever the soldiers went. The soldiers also carried instant coffee. This strategic intertwining of corporate and national interests meant that the US government tacitly supported Coca-Cola's global expansion, and gave Coca-Cola a near monopoly with US soldiers. By the end of World War II, Coca-Cola and instant coffee had become synonymous with the USA in the minds of US soldiers and their international allies (Mintz 1996; Weiner 2002). In the postwar years, both products experienced global growth, in part because of the products' positive associations built during the war years. But ironically, the same thing happened in Axis countries, because the Coca-Cola bottling company in Germany successfully presented itself as inherently German during the war. One of Coca-Cola's great claims is that it becomes "local" wherever it goes (Pendergrast 2000). But in the ironies of global interconnections, the identification with American values that enhance Coke's popularity has simultaneously made it a lightening rod for those who oppose the downsides of American adherence to unconstrained capitalism, materialism, and individualism. Starbucks has excited similar sentiments. Each company has been vilified locally as a global interloper and globally as a threat to local traditions and cultural coherence.

Anthropological studies of Coca-Cola and other products have found that despite the risks that Coca-Cola poses for local communities, it can also affirm culture and community, or be used in novel ways (Foster 2008). For example, Coca-Cola became linked to the American Civil Rights Movement in the minds of young blacks when they were denied the right to buy a Coke at soda fountains. The experience represented a clear violation of their rights, because they had been refused something that belonged to every American (Weiner 2002). As this example illustrates, symbolic and practical dimensions of commodities can take on multiple meanings and interpretations as individuals and groups incorporate them into their lives.

The competition between coffee and soft drinks in the USA may have strengthened both. The American beverage market has grown considerably, because Americans are drinking more beverages now than in the past. Compared to most other countries, Americans consume more beverages and a greater variety (Fletcher 2006; Mintel Oxygen 2009). In the minds of consumers, the choices of coffee, Coke, or other beverages may not mean sacrificing one for another, but a question of what to drink when.

Consumers have also demonstrated a power to influence product choices and sway the behavior of global corporations. Coca-Cola appears to be responding to critics of its high profits and corporate policies by presenting itself as a good corporate citizen. Its recent "Open Happiness" campaign declares the company's commitment to funding scholarships for underprivileged students. Similarly, consumer interests in specialty coffee, as well as concerns for social justice and environmental sustainability, have compelled TNCs, including Kraft (holder of Maxwell House), to adopt corporate responsibility stances that include purchases of some fair trade coffee. The slipping prestige that coffee suffered between 1960 and the 1990s appears to have reversed. Today coffee drinkers can choose fair trade, organic, and shade-grown coffees because they appreciate high-quality coffee. Or they may see their willingness to spend a bit more as a way of showing solidarity with coffee growers, countering some of the inequities of the profit-driven global economy, and supporting environmental sustainability (Jaffee 2007). "Yuppies" who favor gourmet coffee may also be longing for a more genteel past before mass consumption, and endeavoring to reconstruct a more wholesome era by favoring whole-bean coffees, gourmet shops featuring antique coffee grinders, and diversity in coffee varietals and roasts (Roseberry 1996). Choosing fair trade or other specialty coffees can symbolize resistance to the dominant society. Within punk culture, the choice of fair trade and organic coffee symbolized opposition to capitalism, and rejection of a society characterized by profound social inequities (Clark 2004). In the past 20 years, fair trade and specialty coffees have become the fastest-growing segment of the global coffee market (see Chapters 17 and 18). The success of these coffees in many niche markets reflects associations with social values and meanings held dear by people across a range of social groups and political perspectives. Moreover, the diversification in coffee markets allows better-off coffee drinkers to assert class differences and privileged taste by purchasing higher-priced, gourmet coffees (Fridell 2007)—as Bourdieu would have anticipated. The growth of specialty coffees is also related to the growth of global networks and connections that create relationships among people who probably will never meet each other.

Questions for Reading, Reflection, and Debate

1. Do you drink coffee? Why or why not?
2. Do you drink caffeinated beverages other than coffee? If you don't drink coffee but you do drink other caffeinated beverages, why?
3. In addition to the slogans mentioned in this chapter, what other famous slogans are related to drinking certain beverages or eating certain foods? What makes these slogans memorable?
4. Has a slogan or an advertisement ever convinced you to try a new drink or food? Why or why not?
5. What does Coca-Cola mean to you? What does coffee mean to you?
6. Why is Coca-Cola a controversial product around the world? What do the controversies have to do with American ideals of democracy, citizenship, and "the American Way of Life"?

4

TRACING COFFEE CONNECTIONS

It's a Saturday morning in July at the Bloomington Farmers' Market. I am standing in front of Nick's specialty coffee stand, trying to make a decision. In addition to a selection of brewed coffees and espresso, Nick offers a variety of fresh-roasted coffee beans from around the world. Today he has coffee sourced from 16 countries across Southeast Asia, Africa, and Latin America. Each coffee has a special aroma and set of flavors that result from the combination of soils, microclimate, and processing treatment in the region of origin. I want to buy a pound of coffee to prepare at home for the coming week, but which should I select? Do I want to enjoy the rich, earthy flavors of dark-roasted Sumatran coffee? Or the fruity, complex flavors of coffee from Ethiopia, where each region imparts a distinctive flavor profile? Or perhaps today I'll go with a bright, citrusy Costa Rican coffee? Then I spot bags marked "Peru." It's been a while since I tasted Peruvian coffee; I buy a pound. Then I serve myself a cup of dark-roasted java from the thermoses of brewed coffees. Sipping my coffee, I join the people who walk with a coffee cup from stall to stall, looking for the juiciest peaches, freshest lettuce, and ripest tomatoes.

It is easy to accept without question the amazing selection of coffees from all over the world available to us in a small North American city (Figure 4.1). A fundamental conundrum of food consumption is that food is utterly necessary to survival, yet it is taken for granted (Mintz 2002). In the USA, it is easy to be oblivious to the hows and whats of our food. In part, our lives have become so full and complex that we do not feel there is time or need to think of food beyond its packaging and how efficiently we can prepare it. We also have been encouraged to ignore the background and origins of food by business conglomerates that process and distribute our food (Belasco 2002). When people do not know or care about food origins, businesses can acquire and transform food with little attention to health concerns, human rights, or environmental sustainability. Coffee is no different. The processes by which coffee reaches our lips can remain invisible; we do not have to think about the manufacture

Figure 4.1 Bags of coffee.

of agrochemicals, the backbreaking labor of weeding the plants and picking the cherries (coffee fruit) for wages measured in pennies, the gallons of water needed to clean the beans, or the tanks of gasoline used to transport them to the next stage in their global voyage.

Why is it possible to buy coffee from all over the world in a place where coffee does not grow? We know that global market arrangements make it possible, but how does it work, and what happens on the way? By asking these questions, we further consider how global connections influence coffee production. We start by considering the technological and natural resources needed to produce coffee and bring it to our tables. The discussion then looks at some of the social, symbolic, and economic connections and relationships associated with coffee (Parts III and IV provide more details on these aspects in relation to producing and processing coffee and political-economic arenas, respectively). While certain linkages tie the world together, coffee is also a commodity separated from its origins, and linked to disjunctures and struggles. All of these elements contribute to understanding the social, economic, and environmental dimensions of coffee production and consumption.

Linkages to Global Industrial Production of Chemical Inputs

Conventional coffee growers depend on internationally manufactured agrochemicals to produce their coffee. Coffee plants require fertile soils and can deplete key nutrients rapidly; therefore most coffee producers rely on chemical (inorganic) fertilizers to ensure soil fertility. The most important components in chemical fertilizers are nitrogen, phosphorus (as phosphate), and potassium. Nitrogen must be captured in a solid form, usually as anhydrous ammonia, through a chemical reaction that uses natural gas (Funderburg 2001). Potash provides the main source of potassium; most is mined in reserves located in North America, Europe, and the former Soviet Union (IPNI 2009). Phosphate also must be mined, mainly from dwindling reserves in China, Morocco, and the Sahara. The mining operations typically clear the natural vegetation and release contaminants into water and soils. Thereafter, the anhydrous ammonia, potash, and phosphate must be shipped by land and sea to manufacturing plants, principally in North America, Germany, and Chile (ETC Group 2008). The factories process the elements into fertilizer, which is shipped to coffee-producing countries around the world, and transported by vehicles to locales where coffee farmers can buy it.

Many coffee farmers, particularly those with sun-grown plantations, apply pesticides, herbicides, and fungicides. The world's major agrochemical companies manufacture these products in factories located in the industrial nations of the global north and Southeast Asia. Production of these agrochemicals involves petroleum by-products, and generates toxic wastes that often escape into the air and water. Similar to fertilizers, pesticides and related agrochemicals must be shipped internationally in petroleum-fueled vessels and vehicles to reach coffee plantations. The petroleum used in agrochemicals and as fuel is extracted from one of the world's 4,000 oil fields, perhaps in Saudi Arabia, Kuwait, Nigeria, Venezuela, or Russia, and transported to a refinery. The world's largest oil refineries are located in India, Venezuela, South Korea, Saudi Arabia, and the USA (Helman 2010). By the time fertilizers, pesticides, and other chemical inputs reach a plantation, they have incorporated labor, technology, transportation, and fuel drawn from three or more continents, and generated toxic waste along the way.

Production and Processing from the Plantation to the End Consumer

Coffee plantations begin with clearing forests, with implications for biodiversity, soil erosion, watersheds, and climate change. Then farmers must purchase seeds or seedlings. Depending on a farmer's financial resources and national technical assistance for coffee production, the seeds may be acquired from existing plants, or purchased as improved hybrids from national coffee institutes or agribusinesses. Successful coffee production requires a suitable natural environment, adequate inputs of organic or chemical additives, and labor to care for and harvest the plantations. Coffee laborers are among the most poorly paid workers on the planet, earning cents per hour for demanding and sometimes dangerous work. They apply agrochemicals several times a year to improve yields and fend off pests and diseases. In Honduras, a sample hectare of coffee that was planted with a leguminous (nitrogen-fixing) shade tree produced well with 80 kg of nitrogen, 40–60 kg of phosphorus (P_2O_5), and 90 kg of potassium (KO_2). A sun-grown plantation that did not have nitrogen-fixing shade trees would receive more nitrogen. Fertilizers usually combine these three elements in appropriate proportions, and are applied 2–3 times a year. Pesticides may be applied on a schedule or as needed when an infestation is discovered. Common pesticides used on coffee plantations in Latin America include Furadan, Diazinon, Di-Syston, and Thiodan. Furadan is reported to have the highest acute toxicity for humans of the commonly used pesticides; one-quarter of a teaspoon (1 ml) can be fatal for humans, and single grain will kill a bird. It is used widely on soybeans in the USA (FMC Corporation 2009; Harrison 2006). Diazinon and Di-Syston are both listed on the EPA's restricted pesticide list. Di-Syston and Thiodan can be fatal to humans if inhaled, swallowed, or absorbed through the skin. All of the chemicals are highly toxic to marine life, birds, and animals (Bayer Crop Science 2010; EPA 2008; UCPA 2010). Warning labels on the pesticides advise that protective clothing and masks be worn. However, coffee farmers and workers rarely have protective clothing. Pesticide use is associated with illnesses among workers, soil and water contamination, and pesticide residues in green coffee beans (Rice and Ward 1996; Ryan and Durning 1997).

Organic coffee growers avoid the costs and dangers of agrochemicals, but to maintain soil fertility, they need to make and apply organic fertilizers. Organic methods prove safe for workers and the environment, but require more labor and attention to individual coffee plants than applying chemicals.

Once harvested, processing must begin immediately, or the beans will spoil. Typically, a coffee-hulling machine removes the cherries around the coffee bean by mechanical stripping and washing with water, followed by rinsing and soaking in more water. The water becomes contaminated with the decomposing juice and matter from the cherries, which pollutes water when it runs off into streams. The processing equipment (for hulling, cleaning, sorting, and drying the beans) is made of steel and other industrial components. The iron ore and bituminous coal (or other carbon source) used to make steel must be mined. Major iron and coal mines are found in Sweden, Australia, Brazil, India, Russia, and the USA. The mining and processing of these minerals pollute water and produce waste by-products that are difficult to dispose of safely. The steel must be shipped to the factories that make the processing equipment, and then the equipment needs to be shipped to the place where it is needed. Most coffee-producing countries import machinery for processing coffee. Brazil, Colombia, Mexico, and India, however, have become known for manufacturing coffee-processing equipment that they use nationally and export. The equipment operates with motors that run on petroleum-based fuels, except for drying kilns, which often burn firewood cut from remaining forests. Getting that delicious cup of coffee to our tables is not necessarily a safe or environment-friendly process.

Most exported coffee ends up in 60-kg (132-pound) bags for international shipment in large, ocean-going container ships. Green coffee beans can be easily transported, and store well for extended periods when kept dry and cool. Ease of transportation has contributed to the worldwide adoption of coffee. Arriving in the USA or Europe (the major importers), the coffee beans are transported by truck to roasting facilities. Beans undergo roasting at temperatures up to 470°F for about 13 minutes, depending on the darkness of the roast, the quality of the bean and preferences of the roaster (Sweet Maria's Coffee 2010). The most popular method of packaging freshly roasted coffee is in a vacuum-pack bag, composed of polyethylene, nylon, aluminum foil, and polyester (Ryan and Durning 1997). It will maintain freshness better than other options. Trucks or trains carry packaged coffee to local distributors and grocery stores, where most coffee drinkers buy coffee for home consumption. By the time coffee reaches the cup, it has involved an international host of businesses, uncounted actors, and transportation across oceans and multiple countries. More details on the actors and processes of the commodity chain, which ties the producer to the final customer, are discussed in Chapter 16.

Conundrums of Food Knowledge and Representations

The reality of coffee's origins contrasts with typical media representations of coffee-producing countries. Travelogues, advertisements, and photographs splashed on coffee packages show beautiful photos and descriptions of the indigenous and traditional peoples who constitute the majority of the world's smallholder coffee producers. We find it easy to imagine a paradise where people live close to nature and free from urban stresses. One author describes a Guatemalan coffee plantation:

> The farm is almost intolerably beautiful, covered with the green glossy leaves of the coffee trees, prehistoric tree ferns and Spanish daggers along the roadside (to prevent erosion), rolling hills, invisible harvesters singing and calling to one another, laughter of children, birds chirruping, clouds rolling over tops of hills, big shade trees dappling hillsides, springs and streams.
>
> (Pendergrast 1999:xii)

The description juxtaposes the plantation's "intolerable beauty" with the incessant labor of the workers, who appear as happy, healthy, and unbowed by their toil. Coffee-producing regions may have some of the most beautiful landscapes on the planet, but coffee pickers imagine another version of paradise away from the exhausting work that fills their hours, days, and years. After living in and visiting coffee-producing communities across two decades, I cannot count the times that people have asked me about my country, and asked how to obtain a visa. They hope for a place where work is easy, wages are high, and food is abundant. Coffee drinkers' imaginings of tropical plantations inhabited by happy workers contrast with coffee pickers' dreams of shining cities and pockets full of cash. It seems in all corners of the world, we want to believe that the "grass is greener" and life is better on the "other side." It is hard to conceive of the transformed perceptions that come with experiencing the other side, when stunning green mountainsides reveal grinding poverty, and awe-inspiring cityscapes expose grime, pollution, and inequality.

Physical, Symbolic, and Economic Dimensions of Coffee Connections

The discussion of global linkages above points out that coffee (and many other foods) carries unseen economic and environmental ramifications that are difficult to conceptualize or quantify. The connections go even further. We are linked physically, symbolically, and economically through the production, distribution, and consumption of coffee. Physically, as we imbibe coffee or bite into a coffee-flavored confection, we ingest the nutrients and qualities of flavor imparted to the bean from the soil and water with which it grew. We consume a part of another place as we ingest coffee. We benefit viscerally from lands and people whose labor brings us the chance to appreciate coffee's unique flavor. We can be sure, when we taste coffee in drinks, ice cream, and confections, that it is truly coffee. Chemists have not yet been able to create a convincing imitation coffee flavor without using coffee derivatives (Pendergrast 1999). Even if we do not drink coffee, we are likely to catch its aroma as we go about our daily lives.

Symbolically, cultural meanings and associations for coffee are manifested in ritual practices. Rituals are "any fixed or stereotyped practice, behavioral pattern, or embellishment that has no evident instrumental purpose beyond communication or symbolization" (Winzeler 2008:146). Coffee is among the many foods that have ritualistic behaviors associated with their preparation and serving, because social groups develop beliefs about "right" and "wrong" ways to do things. Certain steps are necessary to make coffee, such as grinding the beans and combining the grounds with hot water, but people have added symbolic and meaningful dimensions. For example, a traditional Ethiopian coffee ceremony affirms and symbolizes friendship. Guests sit at a table, and the hostess roasts green beans in front of them. Then the hostess passes the roasted beans around so everyone can appreciate the aroma. A brief statement in honor of friendship is offered, then the hostess grinds the beans by hand in a stone mortar and brews them in a pot. The full ceremony lasts over an hour because the process is repeated three times, known as *abole–berke–sostga* (one–two–three) (Allen 1999:3).

Economically, consumer willingness to drink coffee drives the commodity chain. If so many people did not make coffee a part of their daily lives, farmers would not grow it, and businesses and entrepreneurs would not buy, transport, process, and distribute it. The global coffee system has grown and increased its reach as production has risen due to increased area planted in coffee, and greater productivity related to hybrid varieties and agrochemical use. Coffee entrepreneurs and businesses have made concentrated efforts to convince the general population to consume more, and consumers and societies, for their own reasons, have continued to drink coffee or increased their consumption. Consumers have been particularly successful in communicating their interest in specialty coffees, and coffees that carry social and environmental advantages. Demand for specialty coffees has grown while consumption of major brands has stagnated. Even so, large companies have reported record profits from coffee sales. In the process, the proportion of profits retained by producing nations has fallen substantially in the past 20 years. Coffee producers have struggled to gain a fair share of the profits from their coffee, and countries that depend on income from coffee sometimes find it difficult to benefit from the fame of their coffee, or even to protect rights to the names and characteristics that distinguish their products.

Ethiopia's struggle to protect the intellectual property rights to the names of its coffee-producing regions provides a case in point. It illustrates how corporations can compete to control proprietary rights to valuable commodities, and how global connectivities can play out on international and national stages. The Ethiopian government applied to trademark the names Harrar, Yirgacheffe, and Sidamo, each of which has unique flavor characteristics from different regions of the country. Starbucks already had applied for a trademark for Sun-Dried Sidamo, which it initially refused to withdraw. The legal and public-relations battles raised serious questions about the rights of TNCs to acquire and market not only the products but the names of specific places, as well as the role of national governments in marketing. Ethiopia appears to be the first country to attempt to trademark a coffee, and is among the world's most impoverished and strife-torn. Coffee represents 50 percent of its export earnings, and is its only major product with renown on international markets. The government argued that trademarking would facilitate a price increase, and help to build the country's much-needed revenues from trade. Starbucks argued that it would return more of its profits to Ethiopian farmers, and prove to be a better partner for development than the government. While some consumers supported Starbucks, many others pressured Starbucks to desist in its patent claim. Efforts to sway public opinion and the media ensued among Starbucks, Ethiopia, non-government organizations (e.g., Oxfam) and consumer interest groups. After several years, the US Patent and Trademark Office granted Ethiopia the Yirgacheffe trademark in 2007 (Faris 2007). In the meantime, Starbucks' carefully managed image of good corporate citizenship took a hit, and it finally withdrew its claims. Ethiopian coffee farmers were largely excluded from the international political drama, and it remains unclear whether they will benefit.

Coffee and Fetishism of Commodities

Through systems of production and distribution, our choices of food can transform the Earth, and may degrade or conserve the soil and water upon which we depend for sustenance. One result of the modern agroindustrial complex has been to separate people from food production. Many things that we consume, including coffee, come prepared and packaged in ways that utterly disguise or contain very little of its original content. A package of hamburger carries no element that implies a cow; a can of ground coffee represents nothing of the bush and cherry of its origins. Some prepared foodstuffs have more to do with laboratory processes and chemical additives than agricultural fields and pastures (Pollan 2008). Marx (1978:319–329) described this profound separation of the consumer from the producer, and the utter transformation of a final product from the original form, as "fetishism of commodities." When coffee drinkers consume their brew without knowledge or concern for its origins, they deny their connections to any troubling truth of how it came to their table. Because coffee is produced far away from the majority of its consumers, it is particularly vulnerable to these separations. But the growth in fair trade and specialty coffees is an attempt to reconnect consumers with producers. The Slow Food and local food movements that are spreading through Europe, the USA, Canada, and Japan in recent years reveal increasing awareness among consumers that they have lost ties to the producers of their food. This awareness has triggered a commitment to rebuild those linkages. The efforts present a challenge to the dominance of impersonal global markets, and have created opportunities to renegotiate the culturally specific and globally relevant significance of coffee and many other foods.

Coffee's popularity in the present can be attributed to many factors, such as its social and symbolic utility, its economic value and political importance, and its adoption as a preferred beverage across many groups and societies. But all of these factors need to be understood in relationship to global connections and the development of the world economic system. While the origins of coffee precede the development of the modern world system, the use of coffee as a beverage emerged not long before European vessels began exploring the globe. Thereafter, the history of coffee becomes inseparable from the history of colonialism, imperialism, and the rise of global capitalism. To comprehend the importance of coffee today, we must explore its history.

Questions for Reading, Reflection, and Debate

1. Do you have any daily rituals or ritualistic practices? How would you feel if you did not do them as usual?
2. Besides coffee, what other common commodities that are not produced within the USA do you use frequently? Do you have any favorite foods that are originally from other countries?
3. According to the author, how does coffee tie the world together?
4. What aspects of coffee's global linkages create problems? In your opinion, which problems are most serious? What opportunities do you think exist for resolving these problems?

5

COFFEE AND THE RISE OF THE WORLD SYSTEM

That cup of coffee you sip at your breakfast table, desk, or café comes from far away. It was grown in Brazil, Colombia, Vietnam, the Ivory Coast, or one of a hundred other coffee-producing lands on five continents. It is a palpable and long-standing manifestation of globalization. For 500 years coffee has been grown in tropical countries for consumption in temperate regions, linking peoples of different lands and continents by trade, investment, immigration, conquest, and cultural and religious diffusion. There is a world of history in your cup.

(Topik and Clarence-Smith 2003:1)

For many of us, the study of history appears to be unconnected to the experiences and pressures of our lives. It can be easy to ignore that many of the ideas, spatial arrangements (roads, buildings, cities), and material items in our daily existence reveal the actions, inventions, and convictions of people who came before us. The coffee we drink today carries genetic traces of the first beans harvested and consumed, even if we are not exactly sure where or when that happened. Coffee was among the first commodities produced not simply for household consumption, but for exchange. How did this happen? As we explore the early history of coffee, we begin to see that the historical spread of coffee is intimately linked with the development of the global markets and international relationships that we know as the modern world system. The patterns of trade, interchange of ideas, and human migrations (forced and voluntary) that began to emerge over 500 years ago laid the foundation for the evolving interconnections, tensions, and contradictions of today's world. Not only was coffee part of this process; in many cases, desires to expand and control coffee production and trade were primary motivations.

Early Uses and Records of Coffee

Coffee's early history is shrouded in uncertainties. We are not sure when people began to consume coffee; we are not even sure where it first happened.

Most likely, coffee originated somewhere in or near present-day Ethiopia, where undomesticated coffee varieties still grow wild. It spread, or was carried, across the narrow Red Sea to Yemen. The first people to use coffee may have been the ancestors of the warlike Oromo people, who lived on the southern borders of Abyssinia (today's Ethiopia) (Pritchard 1855). According to early European travelers, the Oromo ground the coffee cherry and bean together with animal fat to create long-lasting, calorically dense food balls.

Coffee drinking was introduced to the Islamic world in Yemen by a member of the Sufi order, most likely in the latter half of the fifteenth century (Hattox 1985). The Sufis quickly adopted coffee because it helped them stay alert during their nighttime devotions. From Yemen, coffee spread throughout the Arab world. By the middle of the sixteenth century, coffee had become part of life in Arab society, and traders had begun carrying it to Europe.

Early Struggles to Monopolize Production and Trade

Until the end of the fifteenth century, Europeans depended on long, overland routes to bring spices and valued goods from Asia. The desires of European upper classes to find a quicker, cheaper route set the stage for the evolution of new trade networks. As we know well, Spain financed Columbus' 1492 voyage in hopes of finding a shorter way to India, instead discovering a "New World" of unimagined peoples, goods, and gold. The honor of finding a sea route to India and the Far East's precious spices, tea, and sugar fell to Vasco Da Gama, who found his way around Cape Horn in 1498.

Europeans were not alone in seeking to extend their influence, power, and access to valuable products. In the Middle East, Ottoman Turks expanded their empire from the fifteenth through the seventeenth centuries. They conquered Yemen in 1536, and gained control of the coffee grown in mountain villages. In 1537, the expansionist Oromo people of North Africa invaded Ethiopia and, possibly energized by coffee food balls, fought to increase their land and influence. Ethiopian coffee producers, who had dominated coffee production up to that point, could not meet traders' demands in the midst of war. As Ethiopia's coffee production fell, Ottoman Turks in Yemen took over as the world's coffee suppliers. The Yemeni city of Mocha emerged as the predominant port of the Middle East as it sold coffee to increasingly interested Muslim and Christian societies. Coffee was traded over land by camel routes throughout the Ottoman Empire. Thus coffee became a profitable commodity in the Middle East before Holland and Britain became major seafaring powers (Topik and Clarence-Smith 2003).

The Ottoman Turks tried to protect their monopolistic power over the coffee trade by prohibiting the export of living plants and fertile seeds. Coffee seeds had to be boiled or partially roasted to render them sterile before leaving the country. Maintaining a monopoly nonetheless proved impossible.

Pilgrims and Colonial Powers Spread Coffee in Asia and Africa

Tradition holds that Baba Budan, a Muslim pilgrim visiting Yemen, managed to evade the Ottoman's export ban on fertile coffee seeds by taping several to his stomach and carrying them back home to India. Some time between 1600 and 1695, depending on the source, Baba Budan planted the seeds successfully in the mountains of Mysora in southern India. From there, Muslim pilgrims probably carried coffee to the East Indies. In 1616, a Dutch adventurer smuggled a coffee plant from the port of Aden to Amsterdam, where it was cultivated in a greenhouse. The Dutch first transplanted seedlings grown in Amsterdam to Ceylon (Sri Lanka) in 1658, and in 1688 or 1696, they planted coffee on Java (Ukers 1935; Weinberg and Bealer 2002). The first plantings on Java failed due to earthquakes and flooding, and new plants were brought from Malabar, India. Thereafter coffee became Java's main export crop, and "java" became inextricably linked to the drink. The Dutch became early leaders in coffee propagation by establishing colonial plantations throughout their Asian colonies, including Sumatra, Timor, and Bali. The early history of coffee's spread thus involved thievery, skullduggery, and intentions to gain by appropriating the plant from its origins.

Between the fifteenth and eighteenth centuries, European governments looked to colonies in Africa to provide coffee for growing consumer demand. The French planted coffee in the Ivory Coast, creating large plantations dependent on slave labor. The Germans spread coffee to Cameroon, while the Belgians found spots suitable for coffee in the Congo. The Portuguese established plantations in Angola, and Italians encouraged coffee production in Eritrea. The British expanded coffee planting in Kenya, Uganda, and Rhodesia (Zimbabwe), where they prevented native inhabitants from producing coffee to ensure that British settlers would dominate coffee production. In Tanganyika (Tanzania), local peoples had developed successful smallholder coffee production using native varieties before British and Germans extended their colonial reach into the region. Colonial administrations chose to protect the indigenous smallholder system rather than risk its disruption by allowing European settlers to take over coffee production (Curtis 2003; Topik and Clarence-Smith 2003). Similarly, producers in Ethiopia's remote highlands continued to grow coffee by traditional means in small plantations. The French East India Company brought coffee to the island of Réunion (formerly the Isle of Bourbon) off the coast of Madagascar in 1715 (Ukers 1935). The island had wild coffee plants, but their quality was considered inferior to the imported plants of Mocha origin. The company governed the island until 1758; it granted land concessions specifically for coffee production and required that each concessionaire plant at least ten trees for each worker. The system depended heavily on slave labor (Campbell 2003). In much of eastern and southern Africa, colonial governments chose to support large plantations and used force to obtain labor. For the rest of Africa's coffee-growing areas, with some exceptions, colonial governments allowed Africans to produce coffee independently because smallholder production presented clear advantages. Households with diversified crop systems had greater resilience to survive market fluctuations, and smallholders using intensive methods usually produced higher-quality coffee than large plantations dependent on coerced labor (Curtis 2003). Colonial policies to support smallholder production or coerce labor for coffee plantations created patterns of labor relations and land tenure that underlie the current social tensions and experiences of inequality in present-day Africa. In a similar time frame, the introduction of coffee and sugar into the Caribbean involved international conspiracies and competition to expand coffee production.

Coffee Comes to the Americas

While coffee spread in Southeast Asia and Africa, Europe's expansionist governments and ambitious individuals looked to the New World to further expand coffee production. Curiously, Louis XIV of France did not take much interest in coffee (unlike his descendants). Captain Gabriel de Clieu, an officer in the French Navy, decided to introduce coffee to the French West Indies without official approval. He smuggled a coffee plant to his post in Martinique from Paris in 1720 or 1723. His part in spreading coffee is better known than most, because he left letters documenting his efforts. The popular version of his exploits holds that he was aided in obtaining coffee seedlings by a French noblewoman. That detail does not appear in de Clieu's writings, but he did note that he had assistance in France, and that it took great effort to keep one plant alive during the Atlantic crossing. A jealous passenger, sometimes identified as a Dutch spy, tried to steal the plant, and managed to tear off a branch. During the voyage the ship suffered damage, began to sink, and water supplies were thrown overboard to keep the ship afloat. The passengers had to survive on severely limited water rations, and de Clieu nurtured the plant for a month with a portion of his ration. Upon arriving in Martinique, de Clieu placed the surviving seedling in fertile soil and posted a 24-hour guard. This single coffee plant has been said to be the ancestor of most of the coffee plants grown in the Caribbean and Central America (Ukers 1935). That belief overlooks that coffee had already been planted on the island of Hispaniola in 1715, and the Dutch had apparently introduced coffee to Surinam in 1718. Portuguese entrepreneurs smuggled coffee to Brazil in 1727, while the British planted coffee in Jamaica in 1730. Caribbean planters soon began to compete with coffee producers from the East Indies. Coffee was not introduced to Mexico and Central America until the nineteenth century, but it became a profitable crop soon after plantations were established.

The myth endures of a single ancestral line of coffee propagation, but as coffee spread globally, people chose seeds for specific qualities and suitability to local climates. New varieties emerged through natural mutations and human selection. By the 1800s, coffee plantations around the world encompassed numerous varieties that differed from the first coffee plants (Topik 2003).

Colonialism, Slavery, and Forced Labor

The expansion of Europe's colonial powers, especially Britain, France, and Holland, is inseparable from the growth of coffee production in tropical nations around the world. Coffee went hand in hand with colonialism, and its production required inexpensive manual labor. In the East Indies, the Dutch required coffee production of its subjects and forced local leaders into contracts to supply coffee at a set price (Fernando 2003). The French and British, who gained control of extensive plantations in the West Indies, resorted to slaves brought from Africa who labored in coffee and sugarcane plantations in unimaginably inhumane conditions.

Wherever early colonial coffee production depended on large plantations, the owners relied on slavery or forced labor. Large plantations needed many laborers at low cost, and owners resorted to legal and extralegal means to obtain cheap labor. A class of elite coffee growers emerged in conjunction with large plantations and colonial administrations, and often became a powerful interest group that shaped regional policies and social relationships among different economic classes and ethnic groups. By contrast, where small producers grew most of the coffee, they exercised some independence. For example, peasant producers in Sumatra were freer from Dutch demands and made their own choices; they responded eagerly to British and American offers of cash for coffee. Unfortunately, smallholder producers generally had little access to political arenas, while coffee buyers, traders, entrepreneurs, and colonial authorities often had greater possibilities of influencing policies in their own favor.

The expansion of coffee in the 1600s occurred as the Dutch and British competed to dominate coffee and tea trade through their respective East India Companies. Three wars related to their trade rivalry occurred between 1652 and 1674. Dutch leadership waned after 1700. In 1784, the Dutch lost their fourth war with the British, and were unable to recuperate. The Dutch East India Company dissolved in 1795, and the British East India Company became the world's foremost trading power of the era. The British took Ceylon from the Dutch in 1796, and established large plantations operated by British owners and officials, who depended on coerced labor from southern India. Although the laborers ostensibly received payment, British landlords deducted wages for transportation, lodging, and food. Rather than leaving for home with earnings, laborers became indebted and served essentially as slaves (Kurian 2003).

The Modern World System Emerges

Political intrigues and conflicts over the control of coffee production and trade contributed to the development of the global economic system that continues to evolve today. The major coffee-consuming nations lie north of the equator, and coffee-producing regions lie in the south. The north–south division aligns roughly with the distinction between the world's most advantaged and least advantaged economies, which trace to the historical division between the imperial nations and the colonized regions. Western thinking predicted that economic development would reach all nations and eventually increase general welfare to create a more equitable world.

By the twentieth century, however, the differences between the wealthier and more impoverished parts of the world appeared to be increasing. Economists Raúl Prebisch and Hans Singer came separately to the observation that persistent economic inequities traced to structural discrepancies in trade; they sought economic remedies to restructure global trade to reduce inequities and alleviate poverty (Toye and Toye 2003). Andre Gunder Frank (1966) and Celso Furtado (1976) examined Latin America's economic struggles and saw the inequities as entrenched processes of "underdevelopment" that resisted transformation. Their ideas became the foundation for dependency theory and its kin, world systems theory. Both approaches agreed that the development of global trade had fostered an inequitable economic system.

Core or "center" areas, at first Britain, France, and Holland, had strong, centralized governments and benefited the most from trade relationships. They came to dominate the global economy between the sixteenth and nineteenth centuries by managing the acquisition and transportation of valuable raw goods, and processing them into refined or manufactured products. The regions of the economic "periphery" lacked strong governments, and were compelled to provide raw goods at low prices to the core regions. The semi-periphery included regions endeavoring to increase their presence in trade between core and periphery areas, but did not rival the economic power of the core. Some parts of the world, known as external areas, initially maintained relative isolation from the emerging economic system (Wallerstein 1980). World systems theorists, including Immanuel Wallerstein and Peter Worsley, recognized that as the economic system evolved new core areas emerged, and external areas become integrated into global economic relationships. Wallerstein's world systems theory saw the global economic system as an integrating whole, but Worsley argued that the emergence of global economic relationships did not create an integrated system. Rather, the evolution of international trade created three "worlds"—first, second, and third worlds—whose diverse cultures, internal conditions, and external linkages shaped their options (Worsley 1990). Dependency theorists argued that these inequities produced and propagated paternalistic (dependent) relationships, in which less-developed countries came to rely on dominant countries for trade and political patronage. Their dependency kept them from overcoming social problems and strengthening their economies.

The emergence of global economic inequities through the evolution of trading patterns has been well supported by examining the history of trade, colonization, and economic processes (Pomeranz and Topik 2006). Yet dependency and world systems theories share a common flaw of failing to acknowledge the variability in local and regional experiences. As even this brief recounting of coffee's spread indicates, individual actions and choices reflect not only global incentives for coffee expansion, but also local conditions. In some places—Jamaica, Martinique, Ceylon, among others—colonial policies granted large landholdings to European settlers, who depended on slaves and coerced labor. In other locations, such as the Dutch East Indies, people were compelled to produce coffee as tribute or to pay taxes. People forced to labor against their will tend to resist and perform as little work as possible, which helps to explain the inefficiency and low productivity associated with early coffee production (Topik 2003). Moreover, dependency perspectives presented European societies and their people as progressive and assertive (as well as exploitative) actors, while other societies appeared passive, static, or unable to change.

Eric Wolf (1982), a noted anthropologist, pointed out that these theories overlooked or underestimated the efforts of ordinary people in the "periphery" to shape their own lives and assert their interests. He used historical accounts to show that people around the world often willingly participated in new opportunities created by trade, and at the same time attempted to resist domination. The example of Sumatran smallholder coffee producers provides a case in point; they participated willingly in coffee production and trade to gain income. Similar to other smallholder producers who adopted coffee voluntarily, they developed agroforestry systems that combined coffee with other useful crops. The diversity of crops provided a hedge against coffee price volatility and helped protect the coffee from pests and diseases that attack monocrop plantations.

Early Connections in an Emerging Global System

Coffee was a locus of early trade relations and colonial expansion. The rapid spread of coffee at the hands of colonial governments and entrepreneurs in Asia, Africa, and Latin America often disrupted traditional cultures and lifeways, and dislocated large numbers of people from their homes. Europe's desire for coffee and other tropical goods transformed the lives of the people under colonial rule, but at the same time, exposure to non-European cultures, peoples, and goods changed European societies. The unequal relationships within and between peoples that were forged in the early days of European exploration and colonization formed relationships that characterize the modern world system, in which political, economic, and trade arrangements systematically favor manufacturing nations and disadvantage nations that produce raw materials, including coffee. A helpful concept is that of path dependence. It recognizes that patterns in sociopolitical relationships tend to be reinforced and renewed through time (North 1990). Power may shift among different interest groups, but the institutions and traditions that undermine or recognize social justice, human rights, and access to resources resist change. Despite the patterns of inequitable relationships that formed between Europe (and later North America) and its colonies, the examination of specific histories shows that local and regional circumstances led to variations in the general pattern (Fridell 2007). The relationships of trade and colonization have powerful influences but are played out in diverse ways on the ground. The growth of dependency was multifaceted, and inequity occurred in European societies as well. Moreover, the societies of Europe and North America became dependent in another way: they became dependent on coffee.

Questions for Reading, Reflection, and Debate

1. If you drink coffee, do you know where it comes from? Or the kinds of labor used to produce it? Does it make a difference in your decisions about whether or not to purchase the coffee?
2. Besides coffee, what other foods or goods are usually produced by southern nations for consumption by northern nations? Besides climate, what other factors influence this pattern?
3. Compare large and small coffee plantation systems. What are the advantages and disadvantages of each? How might higher-level governance influence the prevalence and success of large plantations? Small plantations?
4. Examine readings by Worsley, Wallerstein, and Wolf: What parts of their writings seem to be best supported by the evidence they present? Which aspects seem unconvincing or weak?

6

COFFEE, THE INDUSTRIAL REVOLUTION, AND BODY DISCIPLINE

To drink a beverage is to carry out a small ritual, an act that momentarily constructs a slightly more bearable, intelligible world from the chaos that threatens at all times.

(Jamieson 2001:279–280)

Coffee was known as a beverage or a valuable crop throughout much of the world by the eighteenth century, as trade and exchange linked coffee-producing colonies in the tropics to consumers in Europe. Initially, the upper classes consumed most of Europe's coffee, as well as tea, cocoa, sugar, and rare spices. The ability to consume these exotic imports symbolized not only wealth and the height of fashion, but privileged access to all things foreign (Jamieson 2001). Over the next century, coffee transformed from an elite treat to a beverage for all. How did this transformation occur?

The roots of the transformation trace to several processes, which encompassed growing interest in coffee as a symbol of exotic places, but more importantly to transitions occurring in social and political thought, and technology, which had begun with the Renaissance. Social relationships were also experiencing change with the expansion of merchant wealth, colonial endeavors, and encounters with different cultures and peoples around the world. Moreover, the mercantilist system, through which early traders had controlled trade with monopolistic arrangements, disintegrated as monopolies were broken. Competition among traders brought prices down for coffee and many other goods.

Together these processes set the stage for the Industrial Revolution. As it spread, all of Europe and North America increased their coffee consumption dramatically. The correlation between increasing coffee consumption and industrialization is so strong as to have led some scholars to assert that coffee made the leap from wealthy parlors and coffeehouses to a beverage for the general population because of industrial expansion (Weinberg and Bealer

2002). Others have gone further to suggest that caffeine is necessary to demands of modern capitalism (Wild 2004).

Industrial Production and the Expansion in Coffee Consumption

The Industrial Revolution took off between the end of the 1700s and the mid nineteenth century. Starting in northern England and Scotland, then spreading to parts of Europe and North America, urban areas transitioned to factory production. Factory work demanded alert minds and nimble hands to operate machinery, and the traditional beverages of choice throughout Europe—beer and wine—did not fit these new contexts well. Previously, beer and wine had been safer to drink than most water. Outside of medicinal tonics, hot drinks were basically unknown. The average adult in England consumed weak beer throughout the day, starting with beer soup (prepared with eggs and poured over bread) for breakfast. Beer provided an important source of nutrition (carbohydrates and B vitamins), and most households produced their own beer to meet family needs. A typical English family consumed about three liters of beer a day per person, including children (Schivelbusch 1992). An average person evidently passed the day in a semi-stupefied state from the steady intake of alcohol. Coffee provided a novel alternative, instead of subduing the mind and slowing the body, it enlivened them (Wild 2004).

Important technological innovations facilitated the growth of industry, especially the steam engine, machinery for spinning and weaving cloth, and advances in steel-making techniques. The steam engine, which was adapted to sailing vessels around 1840, proved revolutionary for sea as well as land transportation. Sailing ships had been unable to trade easily with Central America because prevailing winds could keep the ships trapped in harbors for months. By contrast, the outer Caribbean islands benefited from favorable winds and could be visited year round. Coffee became a profitable export for Central America and southern Mexico when steam-driven ships appeared, because they could enter and leave ports regardless of wind direction (Williams 1994). Central American coffee production soared in tandem with industrial expansion in Europe. Prices for coffee, tea, and sugar declined as monopolies ended, and supplies expanded along with increasing demand. Coffee and tea drunk with sugar became a part of daily diets across Europe's social classes. The sweet drinks offered minimal nutrition but provided calories and an energy boost (Clark *et al.* 1995). In France, coffee consumption climbed from 50 million pounds in 1853 to 250 million pounds by 1900, a fivefold increase. In Germany, the 100 million pounds consumed in 1853 increased to 400 million pounds by 1900. Consumption also exploded among the Dutch, Italians, and Scandinavians (Williams 1994).

Emergence of the Urban Working Class

Before the Industrial Revolution, the population of Europe was mainly rural and most people worked outdoors. Between 1801 and 1850, the proportion of Britain's population in cities of more than 50,000 people increased from 15 percent to 29 percent. Although peasants lived in material poverty, they usually had enough calories to meet their energy needs (Clark *et al.* 1995). They obtained food through agriculture, hunting, gathering, and animal husbandry. They grew flax for linen and raised sheep for wool; communal forests provided wood for fuel, construction, and simple furniture. That way of life began to change with the Enclosure Acts of the eighteenth century, which privatized traditional common lands and transferred them to the landed and noble classes. The process displaced the rural poor by denying them access to the natural resources upon which they depended. Reduced access to resources and the possibility of better wages in urban areas combined to push some people and pull others into towns and cities where factory owners needed their labor, particularly in northern England and Scotland where factory production first took hold.

The Industrial Revolution changed the relationship between laborers and the products of their labor, at least in factory work. The transition to cotton cloth from wool and linen replaced the clothing production previously carried out at the household and village level. People produced part of the final product rather than producing something from start to finish, and were paid for performing certain tasks within specific time frames rather than for the product they produced. The factory products were sold regionally, nationally, and internationally; goods became commodities sold without reference to the context of production or circumstances of the laborers (Wolf 1982). In other words, the Industrial Revolution facilitated the fetishism of the commodities for goods that households had once produced for their own use or local exchange. Coffee was already a commodity; it had long been carried to consumers far from its points of origin.

With few other employment options than factory work, displaced farmers and the rural poor became the urban working class. They typically worked in dark, poorly ventilated rooms designed for machines, not for human health or safety. Factory workers had to perform the same task hour after hour, 12 or more hours a day, six or seven days a week (Hopley 2006). People's daily and annual schedules no longer related to a round of activities linked to sunlight and darkness, or to the seasonal cycles of raising crops and domestic animals. Their schedules became fixed by the clock and the demands of industrial efficiency. Industrial production thus transformed the laborer's relationship with the passage of time; it also transformed human relationships with tools and created new relationships with machinery. Factory jobs required people to meet the needs of machines that produced impersonal goods, rather than utilizing tools to create personal goods.

Successful laborers had to perform machinelike motions repetitively, maintain their concentration or risk injury, and ignore the physical aches and stresses that resulted. Overseers and managers similarly had to work within specific time frames and meet deadlines imposed by contracts. Although their jobs were less physically demanding than manual labor, individuals in supervisory or other "white-collar" jobs had to sit or stand for long hours with limited movement. Such large segments of the population had never before been required to keep such rigid, physically constraining schedules. Coffee (and tea in Britain) provided caffeine for workers to wake up and stay alert.

The correlation between the growth of industrial labor and caffeine consumption appears to have developed synergistically. Drinking coffee or tea, with its dose of caffeine helped workers adapt their bodies and minds to a way of living that humanity had not encountered previously on such a scale. At the same time, coffee helped employers and owners to meet their goals of maintaining productivity.

Factory Jobs and Body Discipline

Factory laborers were (and are) subjected to what French philosopher Michel Foucault (1995) called "body discipline." Through their subjection to supervision and the need to function in mechanistic, controlled motions under severe constraints, factory laborers became "docile bodies" to be manipulated by the needs and demands of a hierarchical, industrial society. Body discipline creates a set of expectations that individuals must accept and meet dutifully to obtain or maintain a certain social position. The compensation for factory laborers came in the form of wages and acceptance within their social milieu, but factory labor carried a cost. Individual freedom of movement and expression became limited by the demands of the job. Workers were subjected to surveillance and threat of punishment (loss of employment or wage curtailment) if they failed to perform at set levels of productivity or obedience. Coffee can be seen as an aid to successful body discipline. It also provided a convenient medium for the ingestion of sugar, which became a successively cheaper source of calories and energy during the Industrial Revolution. In Britain, the consumption of sugar (including molasses and syrup) increased from four pounds per person per year in 1700 to 18 pounds in 1800 (Mintz 1986). It continued to climb thereafter. Sugar and caffeine became substitutes for whole foods with high nutritional content, and reduced the time needed to prepare meals among adults who worked long factory shifts. With falling prices for sugar and coffee, the proportion of income that poor households required to meet caloric needs also may have fallen, although nutritional needs may not have been met.

The interesting question is what would have happened if there had been no coffee or tea at the time of the Industrial Revolution? From that time forward, coffee (or tea) became increasingly part of people's lives, and many people use coffee as a way to deal with lifestyles that require long hours of concentrated mental effort. Is caffeine necessary for the modern world system, or is it merely a convenient crutch?

Questions for Reading, Reflection, and Debate

1. What does "body discipline" mean? Where is it found? Have you ever experienced it?
2. What were the reasons for increased consumption of coffee, tea, and sugar during the Industrial Revolution?
3. What foods have become more common or more popular in recent years as compared to your grandparents' childhoods? Why do you think this has happened?
4. How do recent changes in food habits relate to the global system of trade?
5. Why do some argue that caffeine is necessary for the functioning of the modern world system? What do you think?

PART II

ACCOLADES AND ANTIPATHIES
Coffee Controversies
through Time

7

COFFEE CONTROVERSIES AND THREATS TO SOCIAL ORDER

As coffee spread, controversy erupted. More than any other beverage in history, coffee seems to have excited concern, resistance, and even overt opposition as it gained popularity. Coffee historians observe that coffeehouses have been hotbeds of social change in the Middle East, Europe, and the Americas. Why has coffee been such a controversial beverage? Is there a genuine relationship between coffee, coffeehouses, and social transformations?

To explore these questions, the following discussion focuses on the Middle East in the sixteenth and seventeenth centuries, and briefly considers the Revolutionary War of the USA and the French Revolution. The discussion concludes with an effort to answer the questions posed above.

Coffee and Social Critique in the Middle East

Although coffee's introduction in the Middle East occurred in association with religious rituals and medical applications, it was adopted promptly as a social beverage by the general populace. By the sixteenth century, entrepreneurs were selling it in the streets and establishing coffeehouses, which became public gathering places where people of different backgrounds and classes could mix and converse. Middle Eastern society at the time did not offer non-religious gathering places; taverns did not exist because Islam prohibited the consumption of alcoholic beverages, and eating at restaurants was not customary. Therefore, coffeehouses drew people easily, and facilitated a lively social atmosphere that attracted the suspicions of pious leaders and officials. Religious leaders and sects differed on how they interpreted coffee's legitimacy and legality under Islamic law. Its proponents, including members of the Sufi order, emphasized its beneficial attributes of maintaining alertness for long rituals. Detractors pointed out that the Qur'an prohibits the consumption of charred food, and coffee beans are charred by roasting. Other pious Muslims felt that anything new merited prohibition, because the Qur'an did not discuss it. Meanwhile, religious-political leaders became uneasy as coffeehouses became places for social revelry and activities deemed immoral by Islam, including unorthodox sexual behaviors. Crowds in coffeehouses talked freely about social problems and dared to venture political opinions; for many leaders, this was unacceptable.

One of coffee's early opponents was Kha'ir Beg, an official charged with keeping public order in Mecca. In 1511, he discovered a group of people drinking coffee outside a mosque, and to his eyes, their gathering looked suspicious. He moved to prohibit coffee and coffeehouses by presenting evidence before the *ulema* (expert jurists in Islamic law). He argued, with support from witnesses and physicians, that coffee involved problematic public gatherings and caused mental and physical perturbations. Historical accounts differ on whether he was acting alone or under pressure from several other anti-coffee fanatics (Hattox 1985). The *mufti* (a religious legal authority) of Aden argued forcefully in favor of coffee, but jurists decided to prohibit it, perhaps out of fear of Kha'ir Beg. One historical chronicler asserted that many of the jurists drank coffee, but were unwilling to risk Beg's wrath. Beg appears in the records as a rigid and intolerant individual, "someone who was not only too uptight to have fun but was alarmed by evidence that other people were doing so" (Weinberg and Bealer 2002:12). Beg and his deputies proceeded to close down coffeehouses and burn all the coffee they found. His campaign proved short. When the sultan in Cairo, a known coffee drinker and Beg's superior, received a copy of the ordinance, he softened it considerably. Coffeehouses reopened, with the expectation that clients would behave decorously (Robinson 1972).

The sultan's edict failed to settle anything, not even in Cairo. In 1521 and 1532, Cairo suffered riots over coffeehouses. Opponents included people opposed to coffee on religious principles, as well as neighbors who were tired of coffeehouses' raucous noise late at night. In Constantinople, the first coffeehouse opened around 1554, and rapidly attracted a large public that sipped coffee while engaging in a range of social activities—animated conversation, political debate, playing games (such as chess and backgammon), listening to storytellers, and perhaps conducting certain prohibited activities. European visitors suspected that young boys working as attendants also served as prostitutes; however, these travelers may have been predisposed to suspect such behaviors in cultures they found strange (Ellis 2004). By 1570, 600 coffeehouses were reportedly operating in Constantinople (Weinberg and Bealer 2002). Around 1580, the sultan became concerned over coffeehouse goers' making seditious statements, perhaps inspired by his acts of fratricide (he murdered five brothers to consolidate his power). Eager to quiet his critics, the sultan closed coffeehouses on the grounds that coffee beans were charred, and therefore prohibited by the Qur'an.

His successor reopened coffeehouses, in part to regain tax income. The following sultan, Murat IV, became known for his violent and merciless temperament. To impede opposition to an unpopular war, he closed coffeehouses, and ordered that the proprietors and customers be tied into bags and thrown into the Bosporus. Over and over again, as coffee and coffeehouses spread across the Arab-Islamic world, the conjunction of religious, moral, and political challenges posed by coffee consumption led to efforts to prohibit its use, close coffeehouses, and punish its proponents. In all instances, bans proved ineffective or short-lived. Prohibitions might have driven coffee drinking into secrecy but did not stop it. Indeed, coffee became so integral to daily life that women, who could not enter coffeehouses, could claim lack of coffee in the home as a contributing justification for divorce. Coffee remained a topic for religious debate, dissertations, essays, and poems for decades across the Islamic world, but coffee consumption was rarely affected (Ellis 2004).

The Patriotic Drink: Revolution in the USA (1775–1783)

The history of the Revolutionary War ties to the history of coffee in the Americas. The Boston Tea Party occurred during rising resistance to British taxation. The British government had attempted to impose a series of taxes and constraints through the Sugar Act, Stamp Act, Townshend Acts, and Coercive Acts, all of which met with resistance. As every student of US history recalls, many citizens in America's British colonies found it unjust to pay taxes to a government in which they had no representation. Their frustrations culminated in the Revolutionary War and food riots over unjust increases in prices during the period leading up to independence (Smith 1994). Until that time, the colonists had been fond consumers of tea, as well as coffee and cocoa. To avoid paying duties on tea, which had long been in place, colonists had increasingly bought tea imported illegally by smugglers. The illegal trade lowered the sales of the East India Company, and tea accumulated in its warehouses.

The British parliament, acting to advance interests shared with the East India Company, authorized steeply discounted, but additionally taxed, tea prices for the colonies. Parliament expected that colonists would willingly buy the much cheaper tea, and thus put smugglers out of business, increase income for the East India Company, and reduce accumulated stores of tea. More important, if colonists bought the inexpensive tea, they would be paying the tax and capitulating to the government. Patriots saw through this ploy, parliament's move turned patriots against tea entirely. John Warren and Paul Revere published a resolution that vowed to oppose tea sales by the East India Company, and the Continental Congress concurred. John Adams, who was to become the second president of the USA, evidently preferred tea to coffee; he declared that the sooner he could break himself of the tea-drinking habit, the better (Wild 2004). Interestingly, the colonists paid import duties on coffee. It was not merely the tax on tea that spurred supporters of independence to drink coffee. Tea represented part of British culture, and thanks to the parliament, it became a symbol of British oppression.

American coffeehouses offered opportunities for patriots to gather surreptitiously. At that time, taverns served as centers for business activities as well as for social gatherings. In Boston, the Green Dragon Tavern became known as the "Headquarters of the American Revolution." Secret societies including the Sons of Liberty, who evidently instigated the Boston Tea Party, met regularly in meeting rooms at the Green Dragon. Similar to other taverns in the colonies, it served tea, ale, coffee, and cocoa. The instigators of the revolution most likely drank coffee to maintain their focus. It is improbable that they would have chosen tea, which they vehemently opposed. When Paul Revere and William Dawes launched their famous rides to warn that British troops were moving to arrest patriots, they met with co-conspirators at the Green Dragon to discuss their plans. The British did not attempt to close coffeehouses or prohibit coffee drinking; in fact, loyalists frequented coffeehouses sympathetic to the Crown. After the revolution, these coffeehouses embraced independence, sometimes changing their names to reflect newly found patriotic zeal (Wild 2004). The preference for coffee drinking established during the revolution set the stage for the USA to become one of the world's foremost coffee consumers.

Caffeine and the French Revolution (1789–1799)

Less than five years after the American Revolution ended with the British acknowledging their former colonies' independence, French patriots launched the French Revolution. The French cry of "Liberty, Equality, Fraternity" echoed and was to some degree inspired by the American Revolution's "Give me liberty or give me death." Both revolutions arose out of grievances over the political status quo, and involved mobilization primarily among the middle classes and intellectuals who disagreed with inequities propagated by the existing governments. Coffeehouses provided an ambience favorable for learned discussions, impassioned discourses, and political discussions. The Café Procope, among the first coffeehouses in Paris, attracted literary luminaries, including Voltaire, Rousseau, Diderot, and Victor Hugo, and was visited by the young Napoleon Bonaparte. Paris offered a dynamic coffeehouse culture; somewhere between 320 and 600 existed on the eve of the French Revolution (Weinberg and Bealer 2002). Supposedly, the call to revolution and mass mobilization burst from the coffeehouse Café Foy after an impassioned speech by Camille Desmoulins. According to Allen (1999), the storming of the Bastille also has an association with coffee. The Marquis de Sade, who had been imprisoned in the Bastille for 12 years, supposedly begged his jailers for coffee to ease his gastritis but was denied. In furious frustration, the Marquis evidently shouted from his window above the street that jailers were slitting prisoners' throats. The statement held not a bit of truth; the Bastille held only a few aristocrats who had lost the favor of King Louis XVI. The story goes that people in the street heard the Marquis' shouts, and rumors began to spread that the king's opponents were being detained and slain. Ten days later (July 14, 1789), an angry mob stormed the Bastille to free the prisoners. They discovered a large cache of weapons, which enabled the rebels to proceed with the French Revolution (Allen 1999).

Is Coffee a Threat to Social Order?

Why has coffee been such a controversial beverage? This question has yet to be answered definitively. It has been argued that coffee played its unique role because it was new and introduced relatively recently in human history. Although some segments of human societies tend to welcome the new, other segments tend to regard the unknown with caution or fear. Yet, tea and chocolate were introduced to Europe and the Middle East in approximately the same period and did not excite the resistance that coffee experienced. Middle Eastern and European societies did not attempt to prohibit either tea or chocolate. Thus coffee's "newness" may have been a factor, but does not suffice to explain the reactions it inspired. Another possibility may lie in coffee's stimulating effects, but other caffeinated beverages (qat, tea, chocolate) were already available in most places at the time of coffee's introduction. Thus it did not become controversial solely for its novelty or its stimulating effects.

A key factor appears to be coffee's association with a unique context for social interaction, the coffeehouse. For Middle Eastern society, the coffeehouse represented an innovation because it was not explicitly forbidden by Islam as were wine and taverns. With coffee, people could meet and drink together without becoming sleepy or drunk. But why did coffee lead to gathering places dedicated to its sale? This question remains a mystery. Caffeinated drinks other than coffee have not been consistently associated with locations featuring their sale. Tea houses and "tea gardens" have arisen at certain points in history, but they have not had the widespread and enduring appeal enjoyed by coffeehouses. Certain societies nevertheless developed strong preferences for tea, reflecting specific historic and social experiences. Therefore it is not clear that coffee enjoyed any great advantage over other stimulating drinks. By most accounts, it is more difficult to prepare good coffee than tea or cocoa, because the grounds must be separated or "tolerated" with the drink. It is possible that by the circumstances and timing of their introduction, coffee and coffeehouses came to have meanings and associations that distinguished them from potential competitors. The constant factor appears to be an association between coffeehouses and opportunities for social interaction that were not otherwise available at the time of coffee's introduction.

Is there a genuine relationship between coffee, coffeehouses, and social transformations? Historians note that numerous factors contribute to processes of social and political change. The apparent relationships among coffee, social controversy, and revolutions need to be placed within the broad cultural and economic contexts of each time and place. The introduction of coffee drinking, and especially the emergence of coffeehouses, subtly changed the social environment because it entailed a new context for social interactions. Caffeine drinkers tend to become more active and engaged intellectually, in sharp contrast to those who rely on alcoholic beverages for refreshment. The combination of mental alertness and sociality spurred lively conversations, which could turn readily to political debates and social critique. At certain points in history, coffeehouses became places where people had the chance to question authority, challenge preexisting norms and customs, discover new ideas, and foster political action. For people in power at times of social tension, coffee and coffeehouses could threaten the status quo. Struggles over coffee, and social resistance spawned in coffeehouses, recurred through the sixteenth, seventeenth, and eighteenth centuries as entrenched powers and common people experienced economic and political transformations. But it seems unreasonable to suppose that social transformations and revolutions would not have occurred without coffee. Considering the history of resistance, insurrection, and social change, it is clear that people do not need coffeehouses—or caffeine—to oppose injustice, foment revolution, or create new ways of thinking and interacting. In some places, however, coffeehouses appeared at the right time to become incriminated in social tensions and transformations. Thus the apparent association between coffeehouses and countercultural movements may be circumstantial. If so, it was an accident that has repeated itself in many places through time.

Questions for Reading, Reflection, and Debate

1. What are coffeehouses known for in the present? How are their reputations similar to those found in ancient Egypt, Turkey, France, or Britain? How are they different?
2. In what ways is coffee controversial today? Besides coffee, what other beverages or foods have been controversial?
3. How might social issues and concerns influence controversies over foods? For example, how do current societal concerns over obesity trends influence debates about food choices?

8

NATIONAL IDENTITIES AND CULTURAL RELEVANCE

Hundreds of nations and millions of people produce or consume coffee. But what it means to people varies greatly, and the meanings and values associated with coffee are not related clearly to how much is produced or consumed. In some places, coffee has become so integral to daily life that it has become part of national identity. In other places, coffee has been little more than a habit or necessity of life, and in some places, coffee has been overlooked or rejected. Why do these differences exist? This chapter contrasts two producing countries, Brazil and Colombia, and two consuming countries, Britain and Germany, to illustrate how different historical contexts and processes have led to different degrees of national identification with coffee. All of these countries have some common elements that appear to be conducive for embracing coffee as part of national identity. Brazil and Colombia held the positions of the world's first- and second-largest producers of coffee throughout the twentieth century (Vietnam pushed Colombia to third place at the dawn of the twenty-first century). Colombia's global fame and national identity has been closely tied to its reputation for producing high-quality arabica coffee, which is the more valuable of the two commercially produced species of coffee; the other is robusta. Brazil produces more coffee than any other nation in the world, but its global reputation and national identity ignore coffee. Britain had an early infatuation with coffee, but turned into one of the world's most famous tea-drinking nations. Germany accepted coffee later than its neighbors in Western Europe, but today it is among the world's foremost coffee-importing and -consuming nations. Yet Germans retain greater fame and affection for beer. Scholars looking at these differences have explored cultural, economic, and political factors but generally concur that no single factor determines whether a group or national populace comes to understand coffee as integral to an overarching identity, rather than seeing coffee as simply a crop or a beverage.

National identity evolves in relationship to nation-building efforts. Creating the perception of shared identity is a critical challenge to facilitate the governance and control of large populations, especially because today's nation-states typically encompass disparate socioeconomic classes, multiple religions, and diverse ethnic groups. National identities serve the purpose of uniting people into a common nationality despite differences and tensions that may divide them (Schultz and Lavenda 2009). It's then easier for them to tolerate societal rules and constraints on behavior, and perceive that the benefits of citizenship outweigh possible costs. The formation of national identity is an ongoing process, which typically entails a variety of components (e.g., meaningful symbols, ideas, values, attributes) that can encompass multiple meanings and interpretation, and nonetheless create a sense of shared experience.

Is it valid to ask why a beverage would be a worthy component in national identity? Yes. Nearly all locales and nations identify themselves with certain foods and drinks that carry strong associations. The following discussion uses the four examples mentioned to explore why coffee has become part of national identity in some places, while in other places with apparently similar experiences, coffee has been excluded or overlooked.

Brazil's Non-identification with Coffee

If ever a nation deserved fame for coffee, it would be Brazil. It became the world's largest coffee producer in the nineteenth century, and no country has yet to challenge its preeminence. In the extraordinary year of 1906, Brazil produced 82 percent of the global coffee supply. Until the mid twentieth century, it produced almost 60 percent of the world's coffee every year (Topik 1999). Today, global production has increased as more countries produce coffee, but Brazil still represents about 30 percent of the annual global coffee production (ICO 2009). During the late nineteenth and early twentieth centuries, coffee exports set off a process of vigorous industrial development and economic diversification in Brazil, particularly in the principal coffee-producing states of Rio de Janeiro and São Paulo. Taxes on exported coffee constituted a major proportion of government income; they supported coffee prices, the development of transportation infrastructure, and immigration of laborers from Europe (Pereira de Melo 2003). Yet few people identify Brazil's vibrant, diverse national culture with coffee. Brazil's great authors, painters, and scholars have overlooked coffee as a topic worthy of examination or artistic expression. The reasons for this mysterious oversight can be traced to a combination of factors, including coffee's relatively late arrival as a plantation crop, cultural perceptions of the rural hinterland, the public impression of elite coffee growers, and the social and environmental devastation that coffee plantations left in their wake.

The colonial period of Brazil did not evolve around coffee production, but around sugar and mining. Sugarcane was the first major plantation crop, and its demand for cheap labor drove Brazil's dependence on slavery. African peoples were brought forcibly to Brazil to work on sugarcane plantations, and became integral to the evolution of the nation's nuanced experiences of race and cultural diversity. When coffee plantations took hold and spread into the interior, they exacerbated the demand for slaves. With its reliance on slaves, Brazil delayed the abolition of slavery until 1888, the last country in the Western Hemisphere to do so. Coffee growers then turned to European immigrants, who often paid off their overseas passage through years of indentured servitude.

Coffee was introduced into southeastern Brazil around 1774, and at first became established on cleared lands previously planted in sugarcane (James 1932). Coffee plantation life in the rural interior was contrasted with the sophistication of urban culture; the interior was seen as uncivilized. Plantation owners typically left overseers in charge of their plantations and maintained primary residences in cities. Owners often invested in factorage houses that transported coffee to port cities and financed plantation operations (Pereira de Melo 2003), and thus multiplied their wealth. The children of coffee producers associated themselves with urban society and professions that belied their ties to coffee. The coffee oligarchy became unpopular for autocratic behavior and its pressures on the government for favors, even though it never exercised as much influence as commonly perceived (Topik 1999).

Coffee plantations exhausted the soil and, after a few decades, had to be abandoned and replaced with new land acquired further into the interior. Thus coffee was a transitory phenomenon in local economies. Moreover, it usually left behind degraded land and impoverished, landless laborers as well as stagnant rural economies (Pereira de Melo 2003). In the popular imagination, Brazilians did not associate coffee with economic development but with disliked coffee barons, the disgrace of slavery, and a backward, devastated interior. It probably did not help that Brazil's coffee developed a reputation for unreliable quality. Well-cared-for Brazilian arabicas competed with the world's top coffees, but many plantations produced low-quality robustas and suffered from the disregard of an exploited labor force. As one scholar of Brazil's national identity stated, "In fact, coffee is treated more as an embarrassment, a stage that had to be endured but needed to be passed through as quickly as possible" (Topik 1999:87). Instead, Brazil's identity emphasizes a common language (Portuguese) distinct from its Spanish-speaking neighbors, its large territory, great cultural diversity (European, African, AmerIndian, Arab, and Japanese), and global presence, in a combination that is uniquely and powerfully Brazilian (Lafer 2000).

Colombia's National Pride of Coffee

Colombia achieved early renown for the quality of its arabica beans; they became a standard against which other beans were measured. Coffee production spread into Colombia from Venezuela and became an important economic activity by 1870. By 1887, coffee represented 40 percent of the value of Colombia's exports; this percentage climbed through 1943, when it reached 80 percent (Ortiz 1999). Only in the latter half of the twentieth century did coffee's contributions to total export income begin to decline as Colombia diversified into alternative export commodities. In contrast to Brazil, where relatively few people owned coffee plantations, smallholders dominated Colombia's coffee-producing sector through the first 80 years of coffee's development. Elites owned large plantations in certain regions; thus at a national level, coffee growers represented a range of socioeconomic classes.

Smallholdings provided a number of advantages in comparison to largeholdings, which evidently helped their persistence as national laws changed to facilitate the expansion of largeholdings and capitalist agriculture in the last half of the twentieth century. Smallholders generally planted a variety of food crops, trees, and useful plants interspersed with coffee; this diversity gave them greater resilience to withstand price fluctuations in coffee markets (Ortiz 1999; Roseberry 1995). Compared to largeholders, smallholders typically organized labor more effectively and kept costs low with family labor. Through careful management, they also received a greater return on capital investments (Stolke 1995; Taussig 1978). Perhaps more important, coffee came to represent the lives and livelihoods of millions of Colombians, and coffee plantations became an enduring feature of the landscape. Under the protection of shade and careful stewardship of smallholders who often gave trees individual attention, coffee did not exhaust the soils as it did in Brazil. Coffee pickers picked each cherry as it fully ripened, which maximizes quality, flavor, and price. Such intensive labor and supervising is easier on small plantations, especially when pickers have a personal stake in the outcome. By contrast, pickers on Brazil's large plantations typically stripped cherries indiscriminately from the branches, mixing overripe and unripe cherries with mature ones.

Colombian coffee growers have been relatively successful in forming a national-level cooperative to defend their shared interests. Starting with a small group of coffee growers, the National Federation of Coffee Growers of Colombia (FNCC) emerged in 1927. It operates programs to support Colombian coffee growers, enforces high standards, aims to protect farmers from price fluctuations, and promotes Colombian coffee. The FNCC created the Juan Valdez logo in 1981, the fictional figure of a stalwart Colombian coffee grower in the company of his faithful mule. While the stereotypical Valdez figure hardly represents Colombia's diverse population of growers, it has served as an effective symbol to promote and build upon Colombian coffee's fine reputation. Such a figure would not work for Brazil, which lacks a common set of standards and quality enforcement, and does not have a global reputation for quality. FNCC includes approximately 570,000 coffee producers, of whom 300,000 are considered to be smallholders; it also provides programs to support the four million Colombians whose livelihoods depend in some way on coffee (FNCC 2009).

Coffee became a source of pride for Colombians and an integral part of national identity as its quality and rich flavor gained worldwide recognition. A large number of Colombians considered coffee to be central to their well-being, labored to maintain its high quality, and occasionally collaborated to defend joint interests in political spheres—although they argued over specific policies. Urban populations recognized the economic contributions of coffee, and embraced coffee as a national beverage that represented a special combination of hard work, commitment to quality, and appropriate use of a mountainous environment that is exceptionally suited to coffee production. These factors interact to produce what some believe to be the world's best coffee. In Colombia, coffee has become a symbol of national excellence.

Britain and the Abandonment of Coffee

The British people developed an early passion for coffee. The spread of coffeehouses between 1650 and 1750 created a context for the mingling of social classes, lively intellectual exchanges, and business transactions. The development of newspaper and insurance companies, such as Lloyd's of London, began in coffeehouses. By 1700, London had around 2,000 coffeehouses, many of which provided space for fledgling businesses that bolstered the economy (Schivelbusch 1992). However, Great Britain turned decisively to tea in the mid eighteenth century. Scholars have pondered whether the population had a different "taste" or cultural factors that convinced them to prefer tea, but no convincing evidence for this can be found. A more compelling perspective arises through examination of the British East India Company's activities, and the structure of British taxes on coffee and tea (Smith 1996).

The British East India Company, chartered in 1600, represented British trading interests. Its ships carried British products to sell around the world, imported goods to Britain, and re-exported goods produced in British colonies. In the process it made a good deal of money, shaped the development of the British Empire, influenced legislation, and exercised authority over certain colonies including parts of India. This "state within a state" had a monopoly on British tea trade from China, which was the world's main source of tea. Not until the nineteenth century did other places become commercial sources of tea. By contrast, most coffee shipments were handled by middle-class merchants. In the contest between coffee and tea for British loyalty, the British East India Company had the advantages of political power and wealth.

The British population learned about tea not long after coffeehouses began to spread through southern England. Tea did not become popular, however, until King Charles II married Catherine of Braganza, a Portuguese princess, in 1662. Catherine's dowry included a chest of tea and title to the colony of Bombay, which satisfied a longstanding British goal to build trade with India. Catherine disdained coffee, and became known for elegant tea parties for the aristocracy. The general populace took note, and her example probably enhanced the desirability of tea as an energizing "sobriety drink." Along with coffee and hot chocolate, tea was served in coffeehouses.

The seventeenth century's scanty records suggest that coffee and tea cost about the same, import duties were comparable, and British consumption was similar. Tea cost more per pound, but tea leaves could be used several times. In 1711 and 1724, Parliament raised the import duty on coffee to nearly twice that on tea. At that time, most of the world's coffee still came from Yemen. It wasn't until the 1730s that the French Antilles and Jamaica began to produce significant harvests, soon joined by Java. British coffee consumption maintained similar levels with tea until tensions between Britain and Spain escalated into the War of Jenkins's Ear (1739–1748). War interrupted coffee shipments, and in 1745/1746, the import duty on tea was reduced. As the price of tea declined relative to coffee, Britons drank more tea and cut back on coffee (Smith 1996). Nonetheless, the British East India Company accumulated excess supplies of tea. Reductions in tea prices as well as tax breaks continued; apparently related to the company's need to move its backlogged inventory.

The Industrial Revolution spurred tea consumption; served with sugar, it became an inexpensive source of calories for the working class (Mintz 1986). Tea also carried the advantage that it did not need to be ground prior to preparation. By the latter part of the eighteenth century, Britain had become a tea-drinking nation, and proudly embraced tea and its rituals as uniquely British. Through the eighteenth and nineteenth centuries, Britain gradually acquired many coffee-producing colonies, eventually controlling Ceylon, Kenya, Uganda, and part of Tanganyika (Topik and Clarence-Smith 2003). Most of Britain's European neighbors consumed little tea, but gladly bought re-exported coffee that came through London from British colonies (Price 1989). It is, of course, too simplistic to credit British fondness of tea solely to its price differential with coffee. Tea gardens spread in the eighteenth century by offering a family atmosphere that contrasted with males-only coffeehouses (Weinberg and Bealer 2002). Tea drinking became associated with gentility, style, domesticity, and civilized manners, unlike coffee's association with intense and sometimes loud debates. Coffee and coffeehouses fell from favor. More broadly, Britain encouraged the populations of its colonies to embrace tea drinking, in concert with the British East India Company's endeavors to sell more tea as plantations in Ceylon and India began to bolster global supplies. But even today, a number of questions endure as to why and how Britain became the lone tea-drinking bastion in Western Europe (Schivelbusch 1992).

Germany's Love of Beer and Coffee

Today Germany is the world's second-largest coffee importer, after the USA, and has one of the highest coffee consumption rates per capita in the world (Coffee Futures Trader 2007; ICO 2009). Germany's love affair with coffee had a difficult and slow start. Coffee came later to Germany than to most of its neighbors—England, France, Belgium and the Netherlands. Coffee arrived in Germany by way of Holland around 1650, and appeared on apothecary lists as a medicinal substance around 1657. Almost a quarter century passed before the first coffeehouse opened in Hamburg, where it served English sailors and merchants. Germans continued their love affair with beer while the rest of Europe embraced coffee, tea, and sobriety. Beer provided a major part of the diet for the peasantry. In contrast to modern industrial brews, traditionally made beer was low in alcohol and contained carbohydrates, vitamins, and minerals. Similar to pre-industrial English laborers, average German men, women, and children drank about three liters of beer a day through the nineteenth century.

Berlin's first coffeehouse opened in 1721 to serve the general public, and thereafter coffeehouses gained popularity rapidly. German doctors found coffee to be a health threat, and declared that it caused sterility, to little avail. Coffee became so popular that King Frederick the Great became concerned that his people were abandoning beer in preference for coffee, which he saw as a poor substitute. In 1777, he issued a proclamation that declared in part, "My people must drink beer. His Majesty was brought up on beer, and so were his ancestors, and his officers" (Ukers 1935:42). Historians suspect that Frederick's primary concern was not his people's welfare, but the expense of importing coffee. Germany was a minor player in the colonial era; it did not have colonies to provide coffee for the country. Therefore Germany had to import coffee at considerable expense from its neighbors. Frederick attempted to end coffee consumption among the general populace, but he supported coffee drinking among the Prussian upper classes. He created a monopoly on coffee, and issued permits to roast coffee solely to members of the upper class. Frederick made a fortune by controlling coffee sales. Common people endeavored to obtain coffee by stealth, but the monarchy enlisted former soldiers as "coffee sniffers" to report and fine anyone caught roasting coffee without a permit. This highly unpopular move compelled commoners to substitute roasted chicory when they couldn't find a way to drink coffee without being caught. The elite openly consumed coffee, which probably increased its demand among the lower classes and its popularity on the black market. By the end of the nineteenth century, the legal constraints on public coffee consumption evaporated (Ukers 1935; Weinberg and Bealer 2002). Today coffee is one of Germany's preferred beverages, and through much of the latter half of the twentieth century, businesses closed for an hour in the afternoon for a coffee break. Germans introduced *Kaffeeklatsches*, coffee cake, and filtered coffee to the world, and yet coffee seems of minor importance to German identity. Beer, however, retains a special place in German hearts and minds.

What Determines the Integration of Coffee into National Identity?

The examples of these four nations only touch the surface of the great diversity that exists in how national identities have integrated or rejected coffee as a representative characteristic. These examples show that no single factor will predict whether something—even a humble drink—will become part of a nation's identity. It takes multiple, interacting dimensions through time, which may or may not include economic costs and benefits, government policies, social popularity, or power and pressure of the elite. Ultimately, national identities incorporate elements that resonate (or can be made to resonate) with a broad swath of the population, and their economic, social, and political contexts.

Questions for Reading, Reflection, and Debate

1. What foods or drinks would you consider to be part of the USA's national identity?
2. Is coffee part of your national identity? Is it part of your individual identity? Why or why not?
3. What other countries in the world do you think of as having national identities that include coffee?
4. Juan Valdez is described as a stereotypical figure. What makes Juan Valdez stereotypical, while Colombia's national identification with coffee is not understood as stereotypical?

9

HOT AND BOTHERED
Coffee and Caffeine Humor

Elise DeCamp[1] with Catherine M. Tucker

Human beings use humor for many purposes, often to explore issues that capture public attention with a wry perspective or thought-provoking twists. It is no coincidence that many of the cartoon collections on coffee came out in the mid-1990s, at a time of rising "caffeine culture." The humor in these cartoons as well as the commercials and collected witticisms that reflect on coffee all speak in some way to the effects of caffeine on the mind, mood, and energy, and the popularity of coffeehouses that arose with the twentieth-century caffeine culture. Modern coffee humor comments on enduring debates and polarized discourses on coffee's and caffeine's effects on the physical, mental, and social well-being of its consumers. Arguments about the physical effects of coffee consumption appear to be wildly conflicting: coffee is praised or vilified for being energizing or addictive, relaxing or overly stimulating, intensifying or inhibiting sex drive (and thus encouraging sin or virtue), and supporting sociality or driving isolation. Why do these contrasting representations of coffee's effects appear reasonable as well as entertaining? Is it possible that coffee consumption has such diverse physiological and social ramifications?

Energizing or Debilitating? Conflicting Experiences of Coffee

A major thread in coffee humor focuses on its caffeine-induced physiological effects. Humorists play on coffee's reputation as a useful stimulant that promotes alertness, increases productivity, and re-energizes the consumer (perhaps too much) (Figure 9.1). This focus on caffeine's effects is not surprising; well before caffeine was chemically isolated in 1819, its stimulating effects on alertness and energy were widely recognized and conflated with the bean and the beverage. Coffee mugs, bumper stickers, and posters have been used to declare coffee lovers' unapologetic reliance on caffeine as an energy booster.

1 Elise DeCamp is a doctoral candidate in Anthropology at Indiana University.

Figure 9.1 "Caffeinated Cow" by Randy Glasbergen, used with permission.

"A morning without coffee is like sleep," declares one bumper sticker; another shows a sketch of a steaming coffee mug with the statement, "My drug of choice." Recognizing the omnipresence of coffee in the American workplace, cartoonists have poked fun at the use of coffee to boost productivity (Figure 9.2). Others have depicted coffee dependency as a comical obsession, going

Figure 9.2 "Coffee Transfusion" by Randy Glasbergen, used with permission.

back more than 200 years. J.S. Bach, a known coffee drinker, composed the Coffee Cantata to make fun of addicts' fondness for the drink and those who dare oppose it. The libretto, by Christian Henrici, tells the story of a concerned father who attempts in vain to end his daughter's coffee habit. She resists, and sings a love song to coffee: "Mm! how sweet the coffee tastes, more delicious than a thousand kisses, mellower than muscatel wine" (Henrici c.1734). Only the father's threat to forbid her from marrying seems to convince her, until she reveals that her suitor must promise to let her drink coffee whenever she wishes.

Coffee jokes and cartoons capture widespread awareness that excessive coffee drinking may lead to unfortunate side effects, including "freaking out," jitters, anxiety, or anti-social behavior, as suggested by a T-shirt warning, "Give me coffee and no one gets hurt." The "Too Much Coffee Man" (TMCM) comic strip focuses on a central character's disappointments, often related to excessive caffeine use (Wheeler 2005). In one instance, TMCM ruefully lists the "four coffee jokes" (Figure 9.3), two of which are (1) "Coffee makes you happy, hyper, and inspired. If you drink too much it can make you feel gross" and (2) "Coffee is addictive. If you're used to drinking it, its absence can give you a headache and leave you tired, uncreative, and sleepy" (p. 136). The cartoon points to the risks of withdrawal symptoms when heavy coffee drinkers' caffeine intake falls.

Physiological Explanations for Caffeine's Diverse Effects

Medical research has shown that the dichotomous representations of coffee as energizing and debilitating can be explained by the way the body reacts to caffeine. As you begin to drink coffee (or any caffeinated drink), caffeine triggers the release of dopamine, a brain chemical. Dopamine stimulates the part of the brain that governs alertness, problem solving, and the sensation of pleasure (Griffin 2008:102). Caffeine also influences the availability of fatty acids and glycogen, a form of blood sugar, used during physical exertion. These relationships contribute to improved performance and endurance among athletes who are administered moderate levels of caffeine, although not in all instances (Lamarine 1998; Nehlig and Debry 1994). Caffeine also constricts blood vessels, which can help alleviate headaches among some people (Harvard Health Publications 2004). For people who suffer from migraines, however, caffeine proves to be a powerful trigger (Buchholz 2002). Among sporadic consumers, caffeine causes physiological responses that include temporary increases in blood pressure, urine output, and gastric excretions. Habitual coffee drinkers do not show an increase in blood pressure (Spiller 1984). Among some consumers, coffee consumption may lead to dependence as dopamine receptors and blood vessels adapt to the presence of caffeine. When denied their normal coffee intake, some coffee drinkers suffer withdrawal symptoms such as a headache, insomnia, nausea, depression, fatigue, muscle pain, irritability, and difficulty concentrating (Abramovitz 2002:28). Withdrawal symptoms vary widely, but are less severe than symptoms found with drugs like cocaine or heroin. If withdrawal symptoms occur, they fade in a few days (Smith and Tola 1998). These medical insights reveal that coffee can be both energizing and debilitating, but it depends on the quantity and frequency of consumption, as well as individual variability in responses to coffee (George *et al.* 2008).

Figure 9.3 "Too Much Coffee Man" by Shannon Wheeler, used with permission.

Coffee as a Stress Reducer?

Some cartoons focus on coffee's ability to reduce stress through its association with leisure time. *For the Love of Coffee: 61 Things Every Coffee Lover Knows To Be True* (Reed 2007) suggests this idea frequently. One drawing shows a coffee drinker who has fallen asleep cradled in a hammock with a cup in hand (Figure 9.4). Another drawing displays a car with the bumper sticker "I Break for Coffee," which plays off the series of bumper stickers that begin with "I Brake for..." (Reed 2007:38). The perception that coffee is relaxing may reflect the use of the coffee break in the USA to take a brief respite from work. In an office, the coffee break provides an excuse to socialize even though the intent is to boost productivity. It appears that people's associations with coffee as a calming, comfort food relate to the social context and how often attendees drink coffee. Cleric Jim Burklo, interviewed for *Clergy Journal*'s regular feature "Cup of Coffee," adds the following perspective:

> Why do more Americans go to church than Europeans?... It is certainly not because our worship is more meaningful. It is because coffee hour is as much a feature of our social landscape, as shopping malls, fast food, and baseball. America is set up in such a way that people need a coffee hour.
>
> (Farrell 2006:22)

Don't worry. drink coffee.

Figure 9.4 "Coffee and Relaxation" by Tara Reed, used with permission.

Medical research has discovered support for the notion that coffee aids in relaxation. A study of 30,000 middle-aged Norwegian men and women revealed unexpectedly that drinking more than one cup of coffee a day correlated positively with a reduction in systolic and diastolic blood pressure (Stensvold *et al.* 1989). A reduced blood pressure implies a lower level of stress, or at least a decrease in the effects of internal and external stressors on the body. A number of studies have shown that suicide rates are lower among coffee drinkers than abstainers. Meanwhile, studies with non-caffeine drinkers show that they tend to be more anxious than those who consume caffeine regularly (Chapter 10). For habitual coffee drinkers, anxiety does not appear to be an issue unless they exceed their normal rate of consumption, or become heavily dependent on caffeine (Weinberg and Bealer 2002).

Caffeinated Love: Sexy or Lonely?

Public and popular media have long been concerned with coffee and caffeine's romantic, sexual, or social effects: (1) coffee as romantic device vs. isolating addiction and (2) coffee as erotic vs. enfeebling. Each of these dualities connects to larger ongoing public debates—some more heatedly contested than others—about whether coffee, particularly caffeine, more often benefits or harms the physical, emotional, and social health of the consumer. Interestingly, disagreements over its harmful physical impact on the body often mask other concerns about its influence on economic interests or social relationships.

Any devotion taken to extremes can cause problems for the devotee. An example can be found in the pictorial story *Coffee: The Bean of My Existence* (Thomas 1995). The main character becomes so obsessed with coffee that he experiences social isolation and pounding withdrawal headaches when unable to afford enough coffee to feed his habit. But coffee need not cause romantic isolation. After all, it is the key ingredient of the casual date line "Would you like to go get a cup of coffee?" Similar to the workplace coffee break, meeting over a cup of coffee serves as an informal way to socialize, but in this case, it involves the low pressure, inviting atmosphere of a coffeehouse. Indeed, the coffeehouse has over the last two decades become a place for romantic encounters as humorously depicted in a cartoon by Stephanie Piro (1996) (Figure 9.5) and as portrayed in sitcoms of the mid-1990s and early 2000s, like *Friends, Ellen,* and *Will and Grace.* In the Nescafé Gold Blend/Taster's Choice 1987–1993 commercial serial, imported to America (1990–1997) from Britain, coffee became the medium for drawing together a man and woman who live in the same building.

While the television suggests an aphrodisiacal dimension to coffee consumption, medical opinions as well as popular humor media have been inconsistent. Coffee has been viewed as a libido enhancer as well as an

Figure 9.5 "Caffeinated Love" by Stephanie Piro, used with permission.

inhibitor of sexual drive and fertility. A sentiment that coffee caused impotence arose in the late seventeenth century, and it was reproduced in medical opinions used to underwrite commercial tea over coffee interests (Weinberg and Bealer 2002). The conviction that coffee lowered males' sex drive and caused impotence gained particular prominence in the "Women's Petition against Coffee," a satirical rant published in 1674. Coffee had become a popular alternative to alcohol consumption in British pubs, but it was largely a men's drink because women were not welcome in coffeehouses. Women saw coffee as a threat to their marriages, because coffee-drinking men stayed out late. They protested in the petition:

> we can Attribute to nothing more than the Excessive use of that New-fangled, Abominable, Heathenish Liquor called *COFFEE*, which Riffling Nature of her Choicest *Treasures*, and *Drying* up the *Radical Moisture*, has so *Eunucht* our Husbands, and *Crippled* our more kind *Gallants*, that they are become as *Impotent*, as Age, and as unfruitful as those *Desarts* [Deserts] whence that unhappy *Berry* is said to be brought.
>
> (Clarkson and Gloning 2003)

Men did not appreciate the insult to their favorite beverage, or their capacity to satisfy their wives. They responded with the "Men's Answer to the Women's Petition against Coffee," stating in part,

> Could it be Imagined, that ungrateful Women, after so much laborious Drudgery, both by Day and Night, and the best of our Blood and Spirits spent in your Service, you should thus publickly Complain?...
>
> ...Coffee Collects and settles the Spirits, makes the erection more Vigorous, the Ejaculation more full, adds a spiritualescency to the Sperme, and renders it more firm and suitable to the Gusto of the womb, and proportionate to the ardours and expectation too, of the female Paramour.
>
> (Clarkson and Gloning 2005)

In recent studies concerning caffeine's effect on fertility, it appears that its effects on sexual performance can be summarized with the traditional aphorism ascribed to alcohol: "A little stimulates; a lot depresses" (Weinberg and Bealer 2002). Most current collections of cartoons and sayings related to coffee and sexuality make no distinction with respect to degree, emphasizing only its ability to spark sexual desire. In *You Know You're Drinking Too Much Coffee When...*, the phrase is completed with such jokes as "you have a bumper sticker that says, 'Coffee drinkers are good in the sack'" and "your lover uses soft lights, romantic music, and a glass of iced coffee to get you in the mood" (Ilan and Ilan 1996:4, 112). Nonetheless, coffee's effect on sexual desire has been a topic for medical research. One study found that 62 percent of female coffee drinkers engaged in sexual activity, while only 37.5 percent of the coffee abstainers reported sexual activity. For males, those who drank one or more cups of coffee a day reported more sexual activity than those who drank no coffee (Flatto 1990:18). The study provides some compelling evidence for stimulation of desire, but it would carry further weight if it had divided users into regular or irregular and light or heavy users because coffee can have a stimulating or depressing effect on sexual drive, mood, and overall energy depending on consumption.

Coffee Humor: A Mirror for Social Concerns

Coffee humor highlights debates over the effects of coffee and caffeine on physical, emotional, and social well-being. Since coffee is often embroiled in political, economic, and social relationships, it follows that it should draw the attention of humorists who subtly critique these discourses while entertaining the publics they address. The dualities of energizing/debilitating, stimulating/ relaxing, social bonding/isolation, and erotic/sexually enfeebling provide commentary on how the public perceives the benefits and risks of coffee consumption. The roots of these apparently contradictory perceptions have origins in the history of coffee, and have ebbed and resurged through time. It is interesting that the caffeine culture that came to prominence during the 1990s paid particular attention to coffee's role amidst the stresses of modern life, including demands for workplace productivity, and the desire for relaxation in a time- and sleep-deprived population. At the same time, twentieth-century humor reiterated ancient preoccupations with coffee's effects on health, sexuality, and social values. Many of the cartoons, commercials, and witticisms communicate the idea that coffee's utility or harmful effects correlate with the intensity and regularity of consumption. This notion finds parallels in academic and public discussions focused on health issues.

Questions for Reading, Reflection, and Debate

1. How is increasing coffee humor related to "caffeine culture"? How does coffee humor reveal modern preoccupations about coffee or other aspects of modern life?

2. Read the full texts of the "Women's Petition against Coffee" and the "Men's Response" (see online resources). What does the content imply about seventeenth-century views on sex and relationships? What similarities or differences seem to exist with present-day society? Does anything about these petitions surprise you? If so, what?

3. Think of a funny joke, cartoon, or advertisement. Why is it funny? What do cartoons and other humorous media suggest about the role of humor in society? Why do you think humans make jokes?

10

IS COFFEE GOOD OR BAD FOR YOU?
Debates over Physical and Mental Health Effects

Coffee has been the subject of medical interest since it came to the attention of Arabian society. Avicenna (980–1037) may have given the earliest written description of coffee's effects: "It fortifies the members, it cleans the skin, and dries up the humidities that are under it, and gives an excellent smell to all the body" (Ukers 1935:8). Early physicians acknowledged coffee's energizing effects and treated coffee as a useful drug (tea and chocolate received similar regard). In the present, coffee has been suspected as a factor in numerous diseases, including nearly every ill of modern society—heart disease, high blood pressure, high cholesterol, cancer, and reproductive problems. Hundreds of studies have examined the possible dangers of coffee through the twentieth century. Many studies failed to reach clear conclusions, and sometimes similar studies examining the effects of coffee on a specific disease or condition, such as high cholesterol, returned contradictory outcomes. More recently, reports have started to suggest that coffee may have advantageous nutritional aspects and reduce the risk of certain diseases.

Why are the health effects of coffee and caffeine unclear and controversial? With such confusing medical information, it is no wonder that people aren't sure whether coffee and caffeine should be considered dangerous or beneficial. What we now know, which was not as apparent even two decades ago, is that studying the effects of coffee presents numerous challenges for medical science. The following discussion examines the complications that have made it difficult for scientists to understand how coffee affects human health. It then considers the risks and benefits that appear to be well supported based on recent research.

Complications in Studying Coffee's Influence on Health

Chemical Complexity

The majority of medical research exploring the effects of coffee on health has focused on caffeine. But caffeine is only one of the pharmacologically active compounds in coffee that may influence human health. Coffee contains a complex combination of carbohydrates, lipids (fats), proteins, amino acids, nucleic acids, vitamins, inorganic compounds, alkaloids, and volatile compounds. In all, coffee contains more than 1,000 different chemical compounds; around 800 are volatile chemicals that dissipate rapidly. Coffee's rich aroma results from the mixture of about 50–60 volatile chemicals released during brewing. Arabica and robusta coffees have important differences in their chemical composition. For example, robusta coffees contain twice as much caffeine as arabicas (Spiller 1984). Studies show that caffeine alone does not explain all of the physiological responses associated with coffee consumption. Decaffeinated coffee appears to reduce the risk of lung cancer among smokers, but not regular coffee (Baker *et al.* 2005). Coffee's chemical complexity has complicated research efforts, and many uncertainties persist about its physiological effects (Esposito *et al.* 2003). It has been feasible to study only a few other compounds in coffee.

Variations in Blending, Roasting, Brewing, and Preparation

The complexity of coffee's chemical composition is further confounded by the many ways that roasters mix coffee beans to achieve desired flavors, making it difficult to test differences that might be related to variability across coffee varieties. The roasting process also affects chemical composition because compounds break down or interact as they are heated for different lengths of time and at different temperatures. Finally, people brew coffee in a variety of ways. Filtered coffee removes most of the fatty compounds in coffee, but boiled, French press, and espresso coffees do not. Early studies addressing the effects of coffee on cholesterol failed to account for the type of preparation. Studies in Europe, whose residents more often consume French press, boiled, and espresso coffees, showed that coffee raised cholesterol. Comparable studies in the USA, where filtered coffee is common, showed little or no association. Researchers sought to explain the differences, which led to evidence that kahweol and cafestol, fatty compounds in coffee, boost cholesterol (Weusten-Van der Wouw *et al.* 1994). This risk is reduced or eliminated by drinking filtered coffee. The lesson is that variations in blending, roasting, and brewing lead to differences in the chemical composition of the coffee, which can be difficult to evaluate or control (Esposito *et al.* 2003). In addition, few studies account for differences in how strongly people brew their coffee, or the amounts of sugar, flavorings, milk, or creamers that may be added. The variations in coffee blends, roasts, brewing methods, and individual additions probably contribute to some of the puzzling results. In other words, all cups of coffee are not equal, and researchers find it challenging to account for and examine all of the differences.

Variations in Individual Physiological Sensitivity

Individual reactions to coffee and caffeine can vary greatly. Drawing general conclusions about the effects of coffee on individuals is problematic when the sample is small, which is often the situation in case-control studies, which match people suffering from a disease to similar people who do not have the disease. Even cohort studies, which follow a large group of people—a "cohort," which is supposed to represent the general population—over time may be problematic because the people who agree to participate may be different from those who do not. Another conundrum is that scientists still lack detailed knowledge of the variability in people's responses to coffee, and how it may influence study outcomes. Much evidence for individual variability derives from studies of reactions to caffeine. While the vast majority of the population tolerates caffeine very well, a small proportion is highly sensitive or allergic to it. Some sensitive individuals experience severe hives or difficulty breathing after ingesting caffeine (Hinrichs *et al.* 2002; Infante *et al.* 2003). Others find that even a small amount of caffeine results in an unpleasant, jittery feeling; they also appear to suffer more sleep disturbances than people with lower sensitivity to caffeine. Caffeine stimulates the brain in ways that can exacerbate feelings of anxiety, and anxious people tend to drink less coffee. Recent research increasingly suggests a genetic dimension to individual anxiety levels, and thus caffeine sensitivity. Personality type can also influence individual responses to caffeine. One study found that at low caffeine doses, introverts responded more dramatically than extroverts on a number of physiological indicators, including higher heart rates. At high doses, however, introverts' responsiveness declined while extroverts showed linear, increasing reactions (Smith and Tola 1998). People who are "supertasters" are three times as sensitive to bitter flavors as the average person. They appear to be more at risk from developing certain diseases because they avoid healthful but bitter-tasting vegetables, like broccoli, as well as caffeine (Carpenter 2003). Variations in individual responses to other chemical compounds in coffee are also likely to exist, and individual physiologies or genetic compositions may shape personal risks or benefits of consuming coffee in ways that we are only beginning to explore.

Flawed Research Designs

Given the many kinds of variability in coffee beans, preparation, and individual physiology and behavior, scientists face many challenges to develop research designs that can isolate the effects of coffee or caffeine on health. A series of studies through the middle of the twentieth century implicated coffee in cancer, heart disease, and other health problems. Subsequent work found that many of these projects had serious design flaws. One type of flaw occurs when researchers fail to control for something that confounds test results. This flaw tends to occur when scientists don't know that a significant association exists between two independent variables, one of which is studied while the other is overlooked. For example, a number of early studies exploring coffee's effects on heart disease and cancer failed to distinguish between smokers and non-smokers. Many smokers drink coffee; smoking and coffee consumption is highly correlated. Initial studies of coffee drinking in the USA showed that study participants had increased incidence of certain diseases, and it was blamed on coffee. When later studies followed smokers and non-smokers separately, it became clear that smoking, not coffee, was significantly associated with these diseases (Harvard Health Publications 2004). Sometimes a research project accidentally excludes a variable that is known to be relevant. One study suggested that filtered coffee could boost cholesterol significantly among some people. The results had to be discarded when researchers realized that they had not accounted for the cream that subjects added to their coffee (Gardner *et al.* 1998).

Design flaws give scientists nightmares. Great effort goes into planning research to select representative samples and control for interactions that may confound results. But because many things remain uncertain about how different kinds of coffee interact with behavioral, physiological, and psychological aspects, it is not possible to control for everything, and design flaws may occur. Fortunately, good science depends on reliable and replicable results. The history of research on coffee and health shows that studies to replicate results can reveal design flaws, and the process of verifying results leads to new discoveries and better understanding.

Evidence That Coffee Contributes to Certain Diseases and Problems

Although many uncertainties endure in assessing coffee's influence on health, coffee does appear to pose risks for a few diseases and health problems among certain groups. To the best of current knowledge, coffee and caffeine present risks for reproductive health, and for infants and children. Several studies indicate that couples who consume high quantities of caffeine have greater difficulty conceiving. Women who consume over 300 milligrams per day of caffeine (more than three cups of coffee) face a greater risk of spontaneous abortion and having babies with low birth weight or unusually fast heartbeats (cardiac tachyarrhythmia) than women who consume less than half that amount. Other studies show no association between coffee drinking and risks to pregnancy or infant development; however, these tended to have few subjects who consumed high quantities of coffee. Given the uncertainties and possible consequences for infants, many doctors advise keeping coffee consumption low during pregnancy (Harvard Health Publications 2004; Winick 1998).

Women with fibrocystic breast disease report that reducing caffeine intake reduces pain and discomfort, and some studies suggest that very high caffeine consumption may cause or exacerbate the disease. Studies of other reproductive diseases of men and women have not produced reliable evidence of associations with coffee (Weinberg and Bealer 2002).

Studies on the effects of caffeine in children have found increased anxiety, nervousness, and restlessness. At high doses, children who are not accustomed to caffeine become more active and vocal. One study followed two groups of children, one group who normally consumed low quantities of caffeine, and another group who normally consumed high quantities. It found that children accustomed to high caffeine intakes reported greater anxiety and seemed less cooperative than children who normally consumed little caffeine. The researchers proposed that these groups of children might have inherent physiological differences that predisposed them to consume or avoid caffeine, but this was difficult to assess (Nawrot *et al.* 2003). Suspicions that caffeine might be related to Attention Deficit Disorder (ADD) generally have not been supported by controlled studies (Higdon and Frei 2006).

Several diseases may be exacerbated by coffee among people with nutritional deficiencies. For example, elderly coffee drinkers with calcium and vitamin D deficiencies face a greater risk of hip fracture. People taking iron supplements should avoid drinking coffee, because caffeine interferes with iron absorption. Certain drugs also interact with coffee and change the body's ability to metabolize caffeine, increasing the chances of caffeine-related side effects such as jitteriness (Higdon and Frei 2006).

Evidence That Coffee May Reduce Risk of Certain Diseases

In recent years, evidence has been emerging that coffee may reduce the risks of certain diseases, especially type-2 diabetes, Parkinson's disease, liver cancer, and cirrhosis. The results were unexpected, and they have received much attention and examination from follow-up studies. Scientific studies are under way to determine how coffee interacts with physiological processes to reduce the incidence of each disease.

The first evidence showing that coffee drinking may reduce the incidence of type-2 diabetes came from a cohort study in Norway in 2002. Subsequently, over 20 studies in the USA, Japan, and Europe have replicated the results, imparting greater confidence that the results are not due to confounding factors. The risks of type-2 diabetes in most studies appear to fall as levels of coffee consumption increase. These results occur most clearly with filtered coffee consumed in consistently high quantities. A Finnish study found that men who consumed boiled coffee were three times more likely to develop type-2 diabetes than those who drank filtered coffee (Higdon and Frei 2006;

Tufts University 2008). Caffeine reduces insulin sensitivity, so it may contribute to coffee's protective effects; however, a few studies suggest that decaffeinated coffee may have a more significant association with lowered risk of diabetes than caffeinated coffee (van Dam 2008). More work is needed to examine the physiological and chemical processes that might explain this finding.

Studies have been fairly consistent in showing that the risks of liver cancer and cirrhosis decline as coffee consumption increases. Researchers are not yet sure why this relationship exists, but they hypothesize that coffee affects the chemical processes in the liver to reduce damage caused by alcohol consumption, hepatitis infections, and other risk factors. A study in the USA involving 120,000 men and women found that risks of death from alcoholic cirrhosis declined 22 percent for each additional cup of daily coffee intake. These results apply only to people with risk factors for liver diseases. Associations appear weak or non-existent for people who reported no liver problems or special risks at the beginning of cohort studies (Higdon and Frei 2006; Homan and Mobarhan 2006).

Over the past 30 years, gradually accumulating evidence suggests that regular consumption of coffee reduces the risk of Parkinson's disease. This illness causes tremors and uncontrollable shakiness; the actor Michael J. Fox is among those who suffer from it. Caffeine's effects on neural pathways in the brain appear to protect neural functions, but precise understanding of the causal mechanism that inhibits Parkinson's disease requires more research (George *et al.* 2008).

Current studies also point out that coffee contains antioxidants that may provide a protective effect against certain cancers and diseases. At least one study showed increased concentrations of antioxidants in the blood of coffee drinkers compared to non-drinkers. Coffee antioxidants may help protect some people from liver cancer, and perhaps other cancers as well. Interestingly, kahweol and cafestol are among the antioxidants in coffee, thus the tendency of these chemicals to increase serum cholesterol needs to be balanced against their possible antioxidant benefits (Esposito *et al.* 2003).

Continuing Uncertainties

Meanwhile, researchers continue to investigate possible associations between coffee and certain diseases. Some of the most puzzling questions revolve around cardiovascular disease. Case-control studies that compare habits of healthy people to those of people with heart disease consistently show an association between coffee drinking and the disease. Cohort studies have not found any associations between coffee consumption and the development of cardiovascular disease (Campos and Baylin 2007). One cohort study that continued for nearly two decades indicated that decaffeinated coffee drinkers were less likely to die of or develop cardiovascular disease (Lopez-Garcia *et al.* 2008).

In several recent studies, ovarian cancer appeared to be mildly associated with high levels of coffee drinking, but longitudinal studies have not found any association (Silvera *et al.* 2007; Steevens *et al.* 2007). Similarly, a few studies of bladder cancer suggested small positive correlations with coffee drinking, but a review of all studies on bladder cancer indicated that the correlation vanished when smokers were removed from the sample (Pelucchi *et al.* 2008). Despite early studies that suggested close causal relationships between coffee and a variety of other cancers, the results proved flawed or could not be replicated (Harvard Health Publications 2004).

Accumulating evidence suggests that there is an inverse U-shaped curve in many kinds of responses to caffeine intake, such that low to moderate intakes show clear influence on certain kinds of physiological and psychological responses, but effects decline or disappear at higher doses. For example, research shows that many people report feeling happier after a cup or two of coffee (less than 300 milligrams of caffeine), but this feeling declined as they consumed more (Smith and Tola 1998).

Ambiguous Intersections of Science and Individual Experience

Despite over 500 years of medical attention to coffee, we still have many questions and uncertainties about the ways coffee influences physical and mental health. Many studies appear to find contradictory results, and often the research has found it difficult to control for all of the relevant variables that may interfere with isolating coffee's effects. Scientists increasingly recognize that genetic makeup and personality type can influence susceptibility to certain illnesses as well as reactions to coffee and caffeine. Studies of coffee have only begun to consider these factors in considering relationships between humans and health. We know very little about how coffee's many pharmacologically active ingredients interact with each other and with individual body chemistry. Caffeine is only one of many potentially important compounds in coffee. More important, individual behaviors (exercise, diet, alcohol consumption, and smoking) and the contexts of people's lives (exposure to stress, environmental contaminants) appear to be more closely implicated with susceptibility or resistance to disease than coffee consumption. Some consensus exists that members of special risk groups should limit their coffee and caffeine intake, especially pregnant women, children, and people who are sensitive to caffeine. Beyond these recommendations, the medical establishment now agrees that moderate coffee consumption is unlikely to be harmful for healthy, well-nourished people who enjoy it. Coffee may even provide protection against some diseases (Harvard Health Publications 2004). Although we still have much to learn about coffee's effects on human physiology, at this point it seems safe to say if drinking coffee makes you feel good and you are not in a high-risk group, then go ahead, enjoy your java.

Questions for Reading, Reflection, and Debate

1. Do possible health risks of coffee consumption influence your decision to consume (or avoid) coffee? Or possible health benefits?

2. Have you ever read a media report about scientific findings that seemed to contradict other reports? What might be the reasons for such contradictions?

3. How do scientists try to prevent or correct for confounding factors when designing and conducting research?

PART III

COFFEE PRODUCTION AND PROCESSING

11

PLANTING AND CARING FOR COFFEE

It's 5:00 a.m. and Fabio and his younger brother Bernardo leave their adobe home to walk to their coffee fields in the mountains. Rain fell in the night, and they slide on the muddy paths as they climb the steep slopes. They turn on a flashlight where the path is carved into the edge of a cliff along a 100-foot drop-off; otherwise they walk in darkness to save the batteries. Dawn breaks as they reach their fields. Earlier this spring, they had cleared land to expand the plantation; they own about a half-acre of mature coffee and plan to double that amount in the coming years. Fabio kneels at the edge of a seedbed where coffee seedlings have grown about four inches high. The seedlings have two leaves (dicotyledon stage) and need to be transplanted before they crowd each other. With great care, Fabio curves his fingers into the earth around a seedling, grasps the stem, and lifts it from the moist, black soil. Shaking off the clinging soil, he examines the seedling; it must have a single, straight tap root to grow into a healthy coffee bush. The seedling passes inspection and he lays it in a tray. He continues to other seedlings, tossing those with crooked or split roots to the ground. Meanwhile, Bernardo fills eight-inch-high plastic bags with soil from a loamy pile; they had sifted the soil to remove stones and roots. He aligns the filled plastic bags in rows under an awning of banana leaves that serves as a nursery, and uses a stick to press a hole in the middle of each bag. When Fabio has filled a tray with seedlings, they work together to place a seedling in each plastic bag and press it gently into the soil. At noon, they break to eat a lunch of tortillas and black beans, reheated over a small fire. When they finish transplanting the seedlings, they water each one with a hose that brings water from a nearby stream. Then they return down the mountain paths, which have dried in the day's heat, and arrive home as the sun sets.

From the time farmers plant coffee seeds, three to five years pass before the plant begins to produce coffee beans. Coffee producers must make major investments of time and resources for several years without any return, and then they must maintain the perennial crop. The significant delay between planting and the first harvest not only constrains producers' income flow, it also contributes to the variability in global coffee supply, and carries implications for the social and environmental sustainability of coffee production. In this chapter, we will examine coffee production and begin to consider the challenges and conundrums that it poses for producers, social relationships, and national economies.

Planting Coffee: Growing from Seeds or Grafting

In the first six months, coffee seedlings need to grow in moist soil and usually do best under even shade. Some differences exist between the two main commercial species of coffee, *Coffea arabica* ("arabica") and *Coffea canephora* ("robusta"). Arabica varieties tend to be more sensitive to moisture and temperature, and grow well from seeds; arabicas represent about 70 percent of the world's coffee production. Robusta varieties, representing the remainder of world production (Eskes and Leroy 2009), are more resilient to weather variability, but grow better when grafted onto a host seedling or established plant. The selection and preparation of seeds or sprouts for grafting requires experience, training, and, if possible, high-quality seeds. Farmers who plant robusta varieties usually start with grafted seedlings in a nursery (Wintgens and Zamarripa Colmenero 2009). Farmers who grow arabicas plant seeds in a seedbed, then transplant the seedlings into a nursery, just as Fabio and Bernardo did (Figures 11.1 and 11.2). In the seedbed and nursery, farmers have more control over moisture and shade to nurture young plants. When coffee seedlings in a nursery have 6–10 pairs of leaves, they can be transplanted into a prepared field to grow to maturity (IHCAFE 2001). Although some farmers plant seeds directly into fields, that method involves more seeds and seedling loss, and requires that farmers weed and maintain a large area of land during germination and early development (Wintgens and Zamarripa Colmenero 2009). Regardless of the method used, planting in a field needs to occur during the rainy season.

Caring for Coffee Plants

To ensure healthy growth, coffee plants need to have adequate water, nutrient-rich soil, and a temperate climate. Coffee farmers carefully select the sites for their seedbeds, nurseries, and plantations, paying attention to soils, wind exposure, temperature variability, water availability, topography, elevation, and risks of pests and diseases. Coffee can grow well on steep slopes, but soil erosion needs to be controlled. While robusta varieties tolerate drought and weather fluctuations much better than arabicas, both will be stunted or killed if temperatures fall near freezing.

Coffee must be weeded regularly to prevent weeds from competing with plant growth and production. Weeding requires manual labor. Use of herbicides greatly reduces the effort required, but workers still must spray the chemical around each plant. The work to maintain coffee plantations continues

Figure 11.1 Transplanting coffee seedlings.

Figure 11.2 Coffee nursery.

throughout the year with weeding, fertilizing, observing plant development, and checking for signs of disease or infestations. As coffee plantations mature, growers must invest extra time trimming bushes and removing dead or damaged branches to maintain an even shape and productivity. When bushes die or suffer excessive damage, they need to be replaced. After about eight years, the productivity of hybrid varieties begins to decline, although this varies with environmental conditions and shade density. If farmers hope to retain production levels, they must prune the plants severely, allowing them to sprout back from the base of the stems. With careful and consistent maintenance, a hybrid coffee plantation can be productive for 20–30 years (Table 11.1). Traditional varieties live much longer, but they produce sparsely and grow tall (2–4 meters). Farmers who

Table 11.1 Steps in Typical Coffee Production and Maintenance

Step	Timing	Comments
Planting seeds		Seeds are planted in a shaded seedbed during the rainy season
Transplanting seedlings	3–6 months after planting	When seedlings have two leaves, they are transplanted to small bags or individual containers
Planting saplings in the plantation	12–18 months after transplanting	Saplings typically are planted in fields when they have 6–8 leaves
Weeding	Every few months for young coffee plants; 1–3 times a year for mature plants	Varies according to grower preferences, labor availability and costs, and the amount of shade in the plantation
Fertilizing	0–3 times/year	Chemical fertilizers are usually administered during critical growth periods, especially right before harvest; organic fertilizers may be applied at any time but usually before and after the harvest
Administering herbicides, nematocides, pesticides, fungicides	0–3 times/year	Used in conventional production but not organic methods
Trimming	As needed	Removes broken or damaged branches and shape growth
Pruning	Every 8 years	Hybrids need periodic pruning to maintain good production; the actual timing varies by producer
Replanting	Every 25–35 years; more frequently if coffee plants suffer damage	Traditional varieties do not require replanting if grown in shade; hybrids have a limited lifespan but survive longer when grown in shade

depend on coffee exports for their livelihood prefer hybrid varieties because they produce much more coffee and usually grow less than two meters high, which makes it easier for pickers to reach the cherries.

The Inevitability of Risk

The decisions about how, where, and when to plant coffee can determine the success or failure of coffee production. Farmers who know their land, the climate, and the soils well, and understand the needs of coffee plants, are more likely to make wise decisions. But farming presents many risks, and there are no guarantees even for an experienced farmer. Even if they make good decisions, farmers cannot control the weather, market prices, or political-economic processes that influence the fate of the harvest and the farmers' livelihoods. More than most crops, coffee experiences volatile prices, and coffee farmers do not know if the prices at harvest time will cover their costs or leave them in debt. Moreover, the best-quality coffee not only depends on the care during planting and growth, but expert treatment during harvesting and processing.

Questions for Reading, Reflection, and Debate

1. What are the main differences between robusta and arabica coffees?
2. What factors likely influence whether a farmer decides to plant robusta or arabica coffee? How does a region's climate influence the decision?
3. What risks do coffee farmers face? What kinds of risks or uncertainties may be greater with growing coffee than many other crops?

12

HARVESTING, PROCESSING, AND INEQUALITY

Amalia and her sister, father, and older brother get up before dawn in the workers' bunkhouse. They fold the two blankets they share neatly on the wooden planks that serve as bunks. They slept in their clothes; each of them has one change of clothing for the two months of coffee picking on Don Tulio's coffee plantations in western Honduras. Their home is a day's truck drive away. Amalia and her family share the bunkhouse, two latrines, and one water spigot with 40 other workers. They jostle with others as they get into the breakfast line. As they walk by the kitchen door, two women are forming and throwing tortillas onto a hot griddle to cook. A young girl hands each worker four tortillas with a spoonful of mashed black beans and pinch of salt on top. Amalia holds out her own plastic cup to another young girl, who fills it with hot, sweetened coffee. Then Amalia sits on the ground with her family to eat quickly before the tortillas cool. They will eat the same thing for lunch and supper. Don Tulio provides food for his workers, although he factors the cost in their wages. As the sun comes over the mountain peaks, every worker picks up a large five-gallon bucket. Amalia ties a bandanna over her head to keep her hair out of her eyes. The foreman breaks them into groups and assigns them a section of the plantation to work.

Early morning mist hangs over the plantation, and dew drips on Amalia's shirt and dampens her sandaled feet as she begins picking the reddest cherries from the bunches of green and ripening cherries that crowd each branch. The branches sag with the weight of ripening coffee. Amalia has to bend over to reach the lowest ripe cherries, and stretch to her toe tips to reach the ones on the top branches. She tries to pick as quickly as possible, without getting leaves, twigs, and green cherries in her bucket, so the foreman won't deduct from her wages. After she fills her bucket, she carries it on her head to the collecting center. She gives the foreman her name as she pours the red cherries into the large receptacle that feeds into the pulping (hulling) machine. She takes a quick gulp of water from the water spigot, then returns to picking cherries. By mid-morning, the mist has burned off and the temperature rises in the sun. Sweat drips into Amalia's eyes, and she ignores the gnats and flies that pester her. She picks quickly; on an average day, she harvests five buckets of cherries. In a good year for coffee prices, she will earn about a dollar for each bucket. In a poor year, the price could be less than 40 cents per bucket. Each bucket she picks is counted by the foreman; she will be paid a lump sum at the end of the harvest. If she needs anything, she will buy it on credit at Don Tulio's pulperia (a small store), and it will be subtracted from her wages. When she pools her earnings with her family for their eight weeks of work, they hope to have enough money to buy fertilizer for their corn and bean fields for the next planting season, and perhaps enough to buy school supplies for her younger brothers, who stayed at home with their mother.

The wages that coffee pickers receive may be their only source of annual income. Workers typically have little education and few employment options. Because coffee growers have many costs, often carry debts, and receive low prices, they find it difficult to increase wages and still make a profit. The average coffee plantation requires about 250–300 work days ("man-days") of labor per hectare (2.5 acres). About 60 percent of the work occurs during the harvest season (Descroix and Wintgens 2009). To get top-quality coffee, each cherry must be picked individually at the height of ripeness (Figure 12.1). A cherry contains two coffee beans (seeds), surrounded by protective layers of skin and parchment. (Figure 12.2). Coffee cherries ripen unevenly across

Figure 12.1 Coffee ripening on a branch.

several months, turning gradually from green to yellow to bright red (except for some varieties that ripen to yellow). As a result, bushes must be picked multiple times as cherries ripen if the owners wish to maintain quality standards and get good prices.

Costa Rica gained its fame for high-quality arabica coffee in part due to a nationwide commitment to careful hand picking and quality controls. Robusta coffee can be harvested by machine; this works in parts of Brazil where extensive plantations grow on flat land. But mechanical harvesting takes all cherries at once—ripe, unripe, and spoiled—along with twigs, leaves, and broken branches. The result is low-quality, marginally palatable coffee that is usually used for instant coffee or in cheap blends. Arabica varieties do not withstand machine picking, therefore the plantations that produce the world's best coffee must be harvested by hand. Without careful hand picking, we would not have good coffee to drink.

Securing labor has been a persistent challenge for coffee production around the globe, in part because wages need to be low enough that growers can make a profit. Throughout the modern history of coffee, the ways that individual growers, and regional and national governments, addressed the labor "problem" has varied greatly (Roseberry 1991). Labor has been obtained

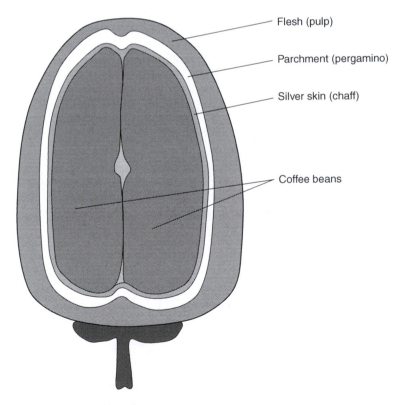

Figure 12.2 Diagram of a coffee cherry.

through slavery and debt peonage, migrant labor contracts, hiring local or regional workers, drawing on family and friends, and combinations of these. Government policies in coffee-growing countries have been developed to encourage or compel people to pick coffee. Costa Rica, for example, has scheduled school vacations so students can pick coffee (Sick 2008). Many factors have interacted to shape how growers obtain labor, including ethnic and social-class relationships, political power struggles, land distribution and availability, and the ways that linkages to markets developed (Roseberry *et al.* 1995).

Smallholders vs. Largeholders: Contrasts in the Organization of Coffee Production

Farmers' options and constraints relate to the size of their plantations as well as the larger socioeconomic and political system in which they live. Producers with more than five hectares of coffee typically are considered largeholders; they may have sources of income other than coffee that allow them to spread their risks. Most of the world's coffee producers are smallholders. They differ from largeholders in the amount of land they control, the quantity of capital they invest in coffee, and their labor sources. Coffee can be produced successfully under a wide range of labor arrangements, property-rights systems, and processing methods. Indeed, the organization of coffee production and its components—land, labor, and capital—have proven remarkably flexible and adaptive to local, regional, and national contexts.

All coffee growers share a need for labor, although the sources and the number of laborers required differ. Farmers with a small plot of coffee often meet labor needs with family, but even they may hire temporary workers during the harvest. Medium to large plantations depend on seasonal labor. Guatemala, Brazil, El Salvador, and Kenya are prominent examples of coffee-producing nations dominated by large plantations, although there are some smallholders. Costa Rica, Colombia, Ethiopia, Papua New Guinea, and Puerto Rico are among the countries where smallholders predominate, although a range of plantation sizes exists. The examples of Costa Rica and Guatemala give an idea of how very different coffee-production systems can emerge despite geographic proximity and similar colonial antecedents.

In Costa Rica, a diversified agricultural sector dominated by mestizo (mixed indigenous and Spanish heritage) farmers emerged prior to independence, and constituted the foundation for a smallholder coffee economy. While Costa Rica shared similar government structures and regulations with other Spanish colonial provinces, it was poorer and more distant from the seat of power in Guatemala. Despite a period of post-independence turmoil and instability during the nineteenth century, the government legislated policies that supported smallholders, granted land titles for those who could show prior claim, and recognized rights to organize, form cooperatives, obtain credit, and make contracts with exporters. A class of small-scale, modestly well-off coffee growers became established, as did a class of landless workers (Gudmundson 1995). A number of coffee growers made their way into politics and worked from elected office to support their interests.

Costa Rica made early moves to establish production standards and facilitate financing through a central bank (Williams 1994). The government declared that picking coffee was a civic duty. Labor was not coerced by force but encouraged by social norms, patriotism, and familial obligations. In the twentieth century, the government started childcare centers in some places to free women for coffee picking. Even so, growers could find it difficult to meet their labor needs; many of their neighbors were too busy picking their own coffee to help. Growers tried to find laborers well in advance of harvest to ensure that they would have enough coffee pickers (Sick 2008). More recently, willingness to pick coffee has declined, along with the importance of coffee for the national economy. Costa Rica has attained one of the highest levels of university education in the developing world. Most young people aim for professional jobs, and migration to cities has reduced the availability of rural labor. Many coffee growers now hire migrant laborers from Nicaragua, who enter Costa Rica as foreign nationals to work for minimal wages with few legal protections. The path of coffee production in Costa Rica, with numerous smallholders who relied on willing rather than forced labor, helped the country to become one of the world's most stable and equitable democracies.

In Guatemala, large coffee plantations owned by elite landowners emerged in the late nineteenth century. They continued a pattern of inequitable land distribution established in the colonial period. As in Costa Rica, coffee growers sought government positions to advance their interests, but unlike Costa Rica, they represented only a small class of wealthy families. Plantation owners needed a labor force, but the majority of the rural population was found in highland Mayan communities. The Mayan people resisted leaving their communities, preferring to farm their own lands. Therefore, the government and wealthy landowners continued tactics begun in colonial times that forced Mayans to migrate seasonally. Through the *mandamiento*, Mayan communities had to provide a certain number of laborers each year to work the plantations. For the people who endeavored to resist or avoid *mandamientos*, vagrancy laws were passed to enable police and landowners to sentence Mayas to forced labor (McCreery 1986). The only way to escape the *mandamiento* was through debt to an export plantation owner.

Debt peonage became the primary alternative for many Mayan people and large plantation owners. Coffee growers wanted the assurance that laborers would return year after year; imposing debt provided the means. Mayan people returned home after the harvest with accumulated debt from purchases made at plantation stores, and an advance against their labor for the next harvest. Mayan people endeavored to make the most of their debt peonage, however, by demanding advances at need; their relationship with labor recruiters provided one of their few sources of cash. Debt peonage released them from forced labor and the risk of capture under vagrancy laws, even as it obligated them to a life of unremitting debt (McCreery 1995).

Through government land titling laws, some Mayan communities lost land, others petitioned successfully to maintain or gain land. Thus the government played communities against each other. By exacerbating tensions and jealousies between communities, the government reduced the risk that communities might unite against the elite (Williams 1994). Mayan communities slid deeper into poverty as populations grew, land became scarcer, and people had few options for employment outside of plantations. Even though *mandamiento* and vagrancy laws were repealed in the twentieth century, the lack of education in Mayan communities has continued to restrict residents' employment options. Poverty and debt combine to draw Mayans to plantations to pick coffee, cotton, or sugarcane. Guatemala became one of the world's least equitable countries in part due to the power gained by a small group of largeholder coffee growers who accumulated wealth by coercing labor.

The Paradox of Coffee Production, Labor Demand, and Development

Coffee growers' dependence on cheap labor creates a paradox for coffee-growing nations and anyone concerned for social justice and human rights. Coffee provides a relatively good, if highly variable, source of agricultural income for rural landowners and governments of tropical countries. But too often profits are concentrated in few hands, and many smallholders and workers remain poor despite their toil and effort. To varying degrees in coffee-growing nations, coffee production depends on the perpetuation of an impoverished rural underclass that depends on coffee production to subsist.

In general, large plantation systems have been more exploitative of labor than smallholder systems. The larger the plantations held by individuals or families, the more likely it is that great socioeconomic gaps and differences in social experiences will create barriers between the coffee growers and the workers. Most likely, laborers on a large plantation interact with a foreman or manager whose primary concerns are to please the owner and compel laborers to work as hard as possible (Figure 12.3). But because growers must compete for labor, they are also compelled to offer labor conditions that will attract coffee pickers. When laborers have choices, they will work for the growers who pay the most, offer better or more food, or provide assistance in the form of cash advances, transportation, or medical care in case of injury and illness. If producers fail to keep their promises, workers find ways to resist. They may allow leaves, twigs, unripe cherries, and gravel to fall into buckets, or damage coffee bushes with careless treatment. Landowners can respond by increasing supervision and deducting wages, but if laborers become upset, they may simply depart in the middle of the harvest, and share their frustrations with other laborers to reduce the landowners' chances of retaining his pickers. They know they can find work picking coffee elsewhere; they also realize that chances are slim that their labor will earn enough to support a better life.

Figure 12.3 Child picking coffee.

Coffee-growing nations face the conundrum of making progress in development while protecting the export income from coffee and, therefore, maintaining an unskilled rural labor force that will work for the low wages that coffee pays. A number of the world's poorest countries are among the most dependent upon coffee, including Papua New Guinea and Ethiopia with 50 percent and 25 percent of their populations, respectively, dependent on coffee production, distribution, or export for their livelihoods (Osorio 2005). And some of the world's most inequitable nations have had rural economies characterized by plantations (not only coffee, but also sugarcane, cotton, rubber, or other commodities) with governments influenced by elite plantation owners, as in Guatemala. The historical example of Costa Rica suggests that it is possible for nations to make economic advances through coffee production. Yet the recent dependence of Costa Rican growers on Nicaraguan migrant labor suggests that Costa Ricans are transferring the social costs of cheap labor to Nicaragua, which has its own struggles to attain economic development. Will it ever be possible for coffee to be produced fairly, equitably, and with adequate remuneration for owners and laborers? Fair trade coffee represents an effort to answer the question positively; its promise and pitfalls are explored in Chapters 17 and 18.

Questions for Reading, Reflection, and Debate

1. Why does coffee require large investments of labor?
2. What kinds of jobs have you had? Would you be willing to pick coffee for the wages that Amalia earns? Besides wages, what motivates you to do a job well?
3. Why are coffee pickers paid low wages? Besides the possibility of fair trade, what else could be done to improve wages? For each possible approach to improve wages, what might be the consequences for coffee pickers? For coffee growers? For other interest groups (TNCs, consumers, independent roasters)?
4. What do you think the chances are that coffee pickers will ever earn wages equivalent to what you have earned? Why?

13

ENVIRONMENTAL SUSTAINABILITY OF COFFEE PRODUCTION

What does it mean to be "sustainable"? The definition most often accepted comes from the Brundtland Commission of the United Nations, which defined sustainable development as meeting "the needs of the present without compromising the ability of future generations to meet their own needs" (Brundtland Commission 1987). The definition recognizes an incontrovertible reality: humanity's survival depends on the long-term availability of natural resources—clean water and air, fertile soil, plants, minerals, and other natural materials integral to human life. Coffee is not critical for human life, but its production consumes many natural resources. Soil erosion and deforestation are occurring in many coffee-producing regions, and coffee plantations contribute to these problems. Given these complications, can coffee cultivation be environmentally sustainable?

Deforestation or Coffee Forests: Sun-grown Coffee vs. Traditional Agroforestry

Coffee originated in tropical mountain forests. Even today, the world's best coffee grows in shade on mountain slopes. Traditional methods of production mimic the conditions found in coffee's original habitat. The earliest methods of planting probably involved creating openings for coffee in the forest understory by clearing out less desirable plants, or introducing coffee to orchards where fruit and domesticated trees provided shade. With traditional methods, coffee becomes part of a diverse agroforestry system that could be called a "coffee forest" (Tucker 2008), in which coffee serves as one of many useful plants for food and other goods. Productivity is low, because traditional methods do not aim to maximize coffee harvests for markets. Instead, they spread farmers' risks and reduce their vulnerability to drought, excessive rain, severe storms, infestations, and market volatility. Short of catastrophic events, traditional agroforestry increases farmers' chances that some of their useful plants will survive despite climatic variability, and provide food or marketable products (Alcorn 1990).

Plantation coffee emerged during the past 200 years as coffee became a global commodity. The spread of plantations contributed to tropical deforestation, because plantations are created by cutting down existing forests. The dramatic clearing of Brazil's Atlantic Forest in the 1800s and the recent devastation of Côte d'Ivoire's forests resulted largely from the spread of coffee plantations (Consumers International 2005). As coffee spread around the tropical world, farmers established plantations with shade appropriate to local conditions. Sun-grown arabica coffee is a recent development (robusta varieties tolerate sun). It emerged in the 1970s, as researchers developed high-yielding dwarf hybrids that could survive full sun, and farmers found that planting the hybrids as a monoculture (one crop to a field) yielded more than shade-grown coffee (Saito 2009). The high productivity of sun-grown coffee led to its rapid adoption, especially among large-scale coffee producers who could afford to replace existing plants, and acquire new forest land to clear for coffee. By 1990, almost half of northern Latin America's shaded coffee plantations had been converted to sun-grown coffee fields (Tangley 1996). In major coffee-producing countries like Colombia, research stations and technical outreach programs propagated the hybrids and encouraged the switch.

I visited coffee plantations for the first time in Colombia in the early 1980s. I saw one plantation with sun-grown hybrids; the squat bushes carried so many beans that their branches could barely support the weight, and the sun beat remorselessly upon the coffee pickers. The experience contrasted with the next plantation I visited (Figure 13.1), where citrus and banana trees shaded the plants. Workers picked more comfortably in the shade than in the sun, and could eat ripe fruit during the day to slake their thirst and hunger. The owner and his family also enjoyed having fresh fruit, and they sold the surplus to local markets. But his bushes were taller and harder to pick from than hybrids and carried fewer cherries; he planned to adopt sun-grown coffee to increase his production.

As coffee-growing regions turned to sun-grown hybrids, unexpected consequences emerged. The removal of fruit trees reduced food availability and variety, with implications for food security. Plantations in full sun experienced higher incidence of soil erosion, suffered more from certain diseases and pests, and required chemical inputs to survive. In some places, sun-grown coffee died off during the dry season, and farmers had to replant shade trees. In Guatemala, the disease *mal de viñas* (a multiple stress syndrome that kills coffee) appears to be associated with sun-grown plantations and perhaps the effects of chemical inputs on the soils (MacVean *et al.* 2001). The greater productivity of hybrid coffee also contributed to a global growth in supply, which contributed to serious oversupply and record-low coffee prices at the turn of the twenty-first century.

Figure 13.1 Shade coffee plantation.

Even though sun-grown coffee has become the standard, many smallholders and poorer coffee farmers have retained traditional coffee plantations or combined traditional approaches with modern hybrid varieties and varying degrees of chemical inputs. In Mexico, for example, a variety of coffee cultivation methods can be found, from coffee grown in native forests, to agroforestry plantations with diverse tree species, to lightly shaded plantations with modest chemical inputs, to sun-grown plantations devoid of shade and dependent on heavy chemical inputs (Moguel and Toledo 1999).

Chemical Inputs: Undesirable, Optional, or Imperative?

Farmers must weigh many considerations in cultivating their coffee, and each involves tradeoffs. One of the more challenging decisions involves the choice of using or avoiding chemicals. Farmers who use chemicals must also decide how much, which to use, and when to use them. For farmers with sun-grown coffee, chemical inputs are imperative. Farmers may start by treating seeds with a fungicide bath before they are planted. Thereafter, hybrid coffee plants grow optimally with periodic doses of chemical fertilizer. Depending on conditions in the local environment and their economic circumstances, farmers decide whether to administer herbicides, pesticides, nematocides, and fungicides.

Chemical inputs, especially fertilizers, increase coffee yields; this is true whether coffee is grown in sun or shade. Herbicides reduce the labor needed for weeding, which is a problem for coffee grown in sun or minimal shade (weeds grow poorly in dense shade). Pesticides, fungicides, and nematocides can reduce losses to insects and diseases. But chemicals shorten the life of the coffee plant, and pose risks for laborers as well as the natural environment (Martínez-Torres 2006). Many of the pesticides used in coffee production have been outlawed in the USA (Cycon 2007). Due to lack of protective gear and sanitation facilities, laborers in unknown numbers suffer exposure to toxic and carcinogenic chemicals (Consumers International 2005). Severe exposure, such as accidental ingestion of chemicals (which may occur if workers cannot wash their hands before eating or if drinking water is contaminated), can lead to death. The chemicals also build up in the soils, flow into streams, and leach into ground water. In some places, water contamination by coffee-processing effluents has led to clean water laws and enforcement efforts, as has happened in southern India (Damodaran 2002).

Although chemical use achieves high productivity in the short term, it is unsustainable in the long term, because chemical use depletes soils of organic material, beneficial microorganisms, earthworms, and mycorrhizae that help to maintain soil fertility. Pesticides eventually become less effective, because pests become resistant. Thus chemical use ultimately reduces yields, degrades the natural environment, and can create "super bugs" that withstand pesticides. One farmer asked me why his insect problems had worsened after he began to use pesticides. He had become dependent on increasingly useless and expensive inputs, but he worried what would happen if he stopped applying them.

Farmers who use organic methods do not apply any chemical inputs, and use shade to shelter their coffee. For farmers who cannot afford chemical inputs, there may be no choice; they are "passive organic." They usually put little labor and investment into their coffee, and obtain low yields. Active organic methods can achieve good productivity, but labor costs increase greatly. Farmers need to mulch, apply organic fertilizers, and perhaps use other natural soil amendments to maintain plant health and boost yields. They may need to compost their own fertilizers and experiment with natural means of reducing infestation and disease. For smallholders who have family members willing to work in coffee production, many of these labor costs can be absorbed without additional expense (Martínez-Torres 2006; Saito 2009). For smallholders without family assistance, and largeholders who must hire more labor year-round to work organically, the increased labor costs may be prohibitive.

Organic coffee production proves to be more sustainable than sun-grown coffee, even though farmers obtain lower yields. Lower annual productivity is compensated by the extended life of the coffee bushes, reduced soil erosion, and maintenance of soil fertility, all of which contribute to long-term productivity and sustainability. Organic farmers save the costs of purchasing chemical inputs, eliminate the risks of exposure to chemicals, and avoid contaminating their water and soils. In addition, farmers may be able to sell organic coffee for higher prices. As chemical inputs have become more and more expensive, farmers have become more interested in organic methods (Plaza Sánchez 1998). Studies in Mexico comparing sun-grown to organic coffee production have shown that organic production obtains higher net revenues due to lower expenses (Perfecto *et al.* 1996). It is not yet clear whether these results hold in other parts of the world.

Advantages of Shade-grown Coffee for Sustainability and Biodiversity Conservation

In many cases, farmers may not find it feasible to adopt organic methods. But shade alone greatly increases the sustainability of coffee cultivation, and reduces the quantity of chemical inputs needed. Shade protects coffee from excessive wind and torrential rains, moderates temperature swings, and increases organic matter and natural mulch through leaf litter. The use of leguminous shade trees, which add nitrogen to the soil, is common in Mexico and Central America. Shaded plantations can produce a variety of fruits, honey, firewood, herbs, and edible plants that can partly compensate for the loss of coffee income when prices fall. Moreover, shaded plantations serve as reservoirs for biodiversity. They often include native tree species as well as domesticated trees. In Central America, researchers found that traditionally managed plantations contain nearly as many species of beetles and ants as native tropical rain forests. Intensively managed plantations with less shade and tree diversity had about half as many arthropods, but sun-grown plantations had only a fraction present (Vandermeer and Perfecto 2005). Shaded coffee plantations provide critical habitat for migrating North American songbirds that spend the winters in northern Latin America and provide biological corridors for rainforest species to move between forest patches (Vandermeer and Perfecto 2005). The biodiversity benefits of shade-grown coffee have led to special certification programs, such as "Bird Friendly®" of the Smithsonian Migratory Bird Center and "ECO o.k." of the Rainforest Alliance and the Sustainable Agriculture Network.

Tradeoffs and Challenges of Shade-grown Plantations

Although shaded coffee has many advantages, it also poses risks and challenges. The amount of shade needed varies with local climatic conditions. Farmers must have intimate knowledge of the local environment to manage shade well and adjust it through pruning, which requires additional labor. Plantations in hotter, drier environments can thrive with dense shade, but in cool, moist environments, heavy shade promotes fungal diseases and lowers productivity. Under certain climatic situations, especially where humidity is high and shade-related diseases occur often, shade-grown coffee may not be viable, and coffee must be sun-grown to produce well.

Shade-grown plantations can have economic consequences. Shaded coffee ripens more slowly than sun-grown coffee. Although this results in a more richly flavored bean, prices in coffee markets tend to peak early in the harvest. Shade-grown coffee can be of superior quality and receive low prices simply because it is harvested later in the season (Tucker 2008). To counteract this problem, farmers have few options unless they can be certified as organic, fair trade, Bird Friendly®, or ECO o.k., all of which promise higher-than-market prices but incur certification costs.

Can Coffee Cultivation Be Environmentally Sustainable?

It is not possible for humans to cultivate coffee without changing forests and impacting the natural environment. But in comparison to annual crops or sun-grown coffee, shade-grown coffee gives farmers a more sustainable option. When planted in the forest understory or under diverse shade trees, coffee can be an environmentally sustainable crop that conserves soil, helps protect biodiversity, and reduces the risks of agrochemicals. The environmental advantages of organic and shade-grown coffee are clear in most cases. The social and economic sustainability of organic and shade-grown coffee, however, continue to be debated. The increased costs of labor, certification expenses, and price risks are among the problems. The next stage in coffee production—processing—has its own set of difficult challenges for environmental and social sustainability, as will be discussed next.

Questions for Reading, Reflection, and Discussion

1. What is a coffee forest? How is it similar to and different from a naturally occurring forest?
2. If you were a coffee grower, what factors would you consider in deciding to plant sun-grown or shade-grown coffee? Which factors would be most important to you? Why?
3. Many environmentalists would argue that coffee cultivation should not be considered environmentally sustainable because of its association with deforestation. What do you think?

14

ENVIRONMENTAL CONUNDRUMS
OF COFFEE PROCESSING

Once coffee cherries have been picked, they must be processed. Although there is a range of variation in the environmental impacts between shade-grown and sun-grown coffee, the choices among processing methods raise additional problems for the natural environment and the possibility for sustainability. There are two main choices for processing: the dry method and the wet method. Producers use the dry method to process robusta coffees. Dry-processed arabicas, called "naturals," can be found where growers lack the technological infrastructure or resources for the wet method. Or they may prefer the dry method due to tradition, as in parts of Southeast Asia and Brazil, which is the world's largest producer of natural arabicas (Brando 2009).

The Dry Method

The dry method involves picking all the coffee cherries from the bushes at once, and letting them dry in the sun. In the simplest dry method, picked cherries are spread immediately on a flat surface to dry. From a perspective of sustainability, this method presents many advantages; it is simple, low cost, generates minimal waste by-products, and requires few inputs other than labor to spread and turn the beans as they dry. Unfortunately, it results in lower quality and prices. Unripe and ripe cherries dry together, and the resulting beans have irregular shapes, unpredictable quality, and may contain small stones and other impurities. The beans may spoil, especially if exposed to rain, humidity, or poor drying surfaces. Often beans are dried on roads, dirt patios, or earth, and surface contaminants can taint the beans' flavor (Martínez-Torres 2006). Problems with the traditional dry method have encouraged additional steps to improve the process. By winnowing the cherries with a sieve, farmers separate out light debris (leaves, twigs, dust). Sifting removes heavier debris, and water floatation separates cherries by moisture content, which greatly increases quality. Brazil uses machinery to dry process its robustas and natural arabicas, but the rest of the world's producers of robustas and natural arabicas use the simple dry process, with some variations. In Honduras, where the wet method dominates, indigenous farmers nonetheless use the dry method and hand sort the cherries that are retained for household consumption. They believe that the bean gains flavor from the cherry as it dries (Figure 14.1). The complex flavors of coffees from parts of Southeast Asia and Africa may result in part from the dry method. Despite the risks to quality, beans processed carefully using the dry method have a full, rich taste ("full body") that is in demand for espresso coffee (Brando 2009).

Since 1990, semi-dry processing has emerged as a compromise between the traditional dry and modern wet method. The main innovation with semi-dry processing is to separate unripe cherries from ripe cherries through a mechanized sorting process with water. The result is a more reliable flavor and better prices (Brando 2009).

Figure 14.1 Sorting beans in dry processing.

The Wet Method

High-quality arabica coffees are processed by the wet method. As soon as the cherries are picked, they are passed through a pulping machine that grinds off the cherry (Figure 14.2). The mucilaginous interior sticks to the raw beans, and must be rinsed off by soaking in water (misleadingly called fermentation). Then the beans are dried. Smallholders usually dry the beans on flat surfaces, such as concrete patios, where they must be turned with a rake to dry evenly (Figure 14.3). Alternatively, they may be dried on screen trays in hothouses (similar to greenhouses) to facilitate evaporation or in large machines that dry beans with warm, forced air. The latter method requires sophisticated, expensive equipment and a fuel source, while the

Figure 14.2 Small manual pulping machine.

other methods require modest investments. Pulping machines range in size from manual machines that a smallholder can operate alone, to elaborate industrial machinery capable of processing large quantities of beans. Sun drying works well on smooth, clean surfaces, but hothouses and machine drying provide weather protection and more rapid drying. Although the wet method produces high-quality coffee, it requires reliable and abundant water, which becomes polluted in the process and runs off into streams and ponds (Brando 2009). It also creates piles of discarded pulp and cherry skins that ferment and decompose into a foul-smelling mess in the tropical heat (Figure 14.4). One six-month study in Central America estimated that the processing of 547,000 tons of coffee contaminated 110,000 cubic meters of water a day (Rice and Ward 1996). Runoff from the wet method causes toxic algal blooms, kills fish, and pollutes streams that rural people use for drinking and washing. Moreover, coffee processing takes place during the dry season when the cherries ripen and water is often scarce.

Figure 14.3 Raking coffee beans to dry.

Figure 14.4 Decomposing coffee cherries.

Mitigating Environmental Degradation in Processing

With increasing concerns for sustainability and efficiency, new technologies are being developed to reduce the environmental damage caused by the wet method. "Ecological" coffee-processing machines reduce the amount of water needed by using it more efficiently, but the cost inhibits adoption. Fortunately, simple options exist to reduce waste and pollution. A retaining pond can be an effective tool to collect water runoff from the processing plant; the pond traps the water and allows it to evaporate. Treating the water with lime inhibits the growth of toxic bacteria and helps to counteract the odor of decomposing matter. In the months between harvests, the water evaporates and leaves a nutrient-rich sludge that can be applied as an organic fertilizer. The discarded coffee cherries can be converted to fertilizer as well by introducing earthworms to decompose it. Earthworms can convert coffee cherries to rich compost when given a moist, sheltered area protected from sun, extreme temperatures, and wind. Thus the wet method can be made more sustainable, but it requires commitment and effort on the part of farmers and processing facilities to reduce waste and recycle by-products.

Can Coffee Processing Be Environmentally Sustainable?

Processing coffee poses more difficult challenges for environmental sustainability than coffee cultivation. While shade-grown coffee provides clear advantages over sun-grown coffee for the environment, biodiversity conservation, and overall coffee quality, the choice between wet and dry methods poses a thorny conundrum. The dry method offers sustainability, but usually at the cost of quality. Despite the wet method's problematic aspects, it will remain popular because most people prefer the flavor of washed beans and market prices respond accordingly. Technological advances in the wet method allow for coffee to be processed with less waste, but these advances cost money and require extra work and commitment on the part of processors. Only a few certification programs (such as ECO o.k.) stipulate that processing must be done in ways that mitigate waste and environmental degradation. Few consumers realize that processing poses risks to the environment, so they do not seek sustainably processed coffee. Producing nations have begun to recognize the risks of water scarcity and contamination associated with coffee processing, but efforts to improve the situation are slow because other problems absorb scarce resources.

Beyond environmental sustainability, coffee also raises issues for social sustainability. The people who grow coffee and care for it often have difficulty meeting their basic human needs; they barely make a living. Most of the world's producers are smallholders; many cannot afford to send their children to school, seek medical care, or buy basic goods. Their real incomes have been falling, and today they receive a smaller proportion of the profits from coffee than ever before (Talbot 2004). For coffee to be successful in the long term, it is not enough for coffee production and processing to become environmentally sustainable. Coffee production also needs to be socially sustainable. The issue is not simply one of morality, but pragmatism. If farmers cannot make ends meet, they will begin to abandon coffee, as happened during the most recent coffee crisis. In addition, social sustainability involves access to basic infrastructure, health care, and education and respect for human rights. History teaches us that repression and deprivation can fuel social unrest, crime, and civil wars Equity and respect for human rights benefit everyone. Social and environmental sustainability, however desirable, present seemingly intractable challenges due to coffee's volatile prices, the way that the modern world system functions, and the current structure of the conventional commodity chain.

Questions for Reading, Reflection, and Discussion

1. Compare the wet and dry methods for processing coffee. What are the environmental and economic advantages and disadvantages of each?
2. Why do you think opinions vary with regard to the impacts of the different methods on quality?
3. The author claims that coffee farmers will abandon coffee if they cannot make a living with it. If smallholders were to abandon coffee, what might be the consequences? How might coffee production and quality be impacted?

PART IV

MARKETS AND THE MODERN WORLD SYSTEM

15

MARKET VOLATILITY AND SOCIAL CALAMITY

In 1999, an unexpectedly large coffee harvest flooded global markets, even though speculators had been predicting slightly lower productivity. Vietnam produced a bumper crop of robusta beans, and Brazil's harvest increased as new plantations, established after a devastating frost in the mid-1990s, came into full production. Around the world, coffee prices slid, and then collapsed. As the bottom fell out of the market, the price fell below the cost of production. In many coffee-growing regions, growers harvested a minimal amount, let employees go, or abandoned their plantations completely. Families dependent on picking coffee had to find another way to support themselves; they migrated to urban areas or across international borders in search of jobs. The greater a country's dependence on coffee, the greater the impact of the coffee crisis. Guatemala and Ethiopia reported deaths from starvation in economically devastated coffee-producing regions (see Chapter 16). Economists debated which approaches could help coffee producers survive, and generally agreed that the future of coffee depended on a global reduction in production of low-quality coffee. International development agencies saw poverty and malnutrition increase dramatically in the countries, including Vietnam, where they had promoted coffee as a means of development and poverty reduction. Following economists' advice, the agencies recommended structural adjustments in coffee production. For nations that had increased coffee production at the suggestion of development experts, the recommendations must have been difficult to digest.

The coffee crisis of 1999–2003 was only the latest in a series of calamities associated with coffee production and markets in the last 250 years. Why are coffee prices so volatile? How has price volatility affected the history of coffee production and the lives of producers? This chapter explores these questions using several illustrative examples.

The Infamous Coffee Cycle

The volatility in coffee markets can be traced in part to two principal characteristics of coffee production. First, supplies of coffee can change significantly over time due to unforeseeable events. Second, the delay of several years between planting and the first harvest makes it difficult to match supply to demand. The combination of these two factors results in the coffee cycle: supply periodically exceeds demand and causes prices to plummet. As prices fall, producers usually cut back on production, leading to lower supplies. When supplies fall, prices rise, and producers plant more coffee, which eventually increases global supplies above what can be sold, and the cycle repeats.

At key points in history, coffee prices and available supplies changed dramatically due to weather conditions, disease outbreaks, and social instability. At other times, falling prices and the social inequities of coffee production led to rebellions and tragedy. During the past 500 years, fluctuations in supply also related to the disproportionate importance of a few major coffee-producing countries—starting with Yemen, then Java, then St. Domingue (Haiti), and most recently Brazil. When their harvests have failed, global market prices have risen; when harvests have been large, global market prices have fallen. Market speculation and national policies also intervened, either exacerbating or moderating the severity of price swings. Struggles among different factions to assert their interests, or simply to survive, also have been recurring issues in the global coffee economy.

Human Misery and the Haitian Rebellion

During the mid eighteenth century, St. Domingue became the world's leading coffee producer. Java and Ceylon, which had risen to prominence during the late seventeenth century, continued to produce important quantities of coffee but became lesser sources. France in particular depended on St. Domingue's coffee, which was produced by slaves on large estates. Slaves, who numbered around 500,000, represented the majority of the population, and endured some of the most restrictive laws ever created by a colonial power. News of the French Revolution helped to spark hope and inspire revolt. In 1791, the slave population rebelled and began a national liberation movement born of suffering and desperation. The conflict devastated the land, and coffee production collapsed. Coffee prices rose, encouraging investment in coffee in the rest of the Caribbean and stimulating Brazil to set a course to become the world's largest coffee producer (Topik 2003; Topik and Clarence-Smith 2003). By 1803, the slaves had gained freedom, and on January 1, 1804, Haiti became the first colonial nation in Latin America to gain independence, and the only nation in the world to have gained it as a result of a slave rebellion. Although the liberation movement involved broad-based participation and support, the process of forming a unified and effective government faltered as the new nation confronted a bitter reality: the rest of the world did not welcome Haiti as an independent nation. The goal of building an equitable and democratic nation has proven elusive.

The Devastation of Coffee Rust

Java held on as the world's second-largest coffee producer through most of the nineteenth century. Along with Ceylon and Indonesia, it provided significant coffee supplies to Europe. Then in 1876, a fungus that causes coffee rust (*Hemileia vastatrix*) spread through Southeast Asia and devastated coffee plantations (Topik 2003). The collapse of coffee production depressed the region's economies and shook colonial governments. Thousands of coffee pickers, a number of whom were migrant workers, lost employment. Many plantation owners abandoned coffee and moved to other crops, especially rubber. The British switched to tea production for plantations in parts of Ceylon and India. In Java, the Dutch government endeavored to enforce rules of obligatory coffee production, but growers hesitated in light of low prices and risks of coffee rust. Peasants resisted plantation work because it interfered with household production (Fernando 2003). Nonetheless, Southeast Asian smallholders experimented with disease-resistant coffee varieties and gradually restored coffee production within complex agroforestry systems (Topik and Clarence-Smith 2003).

Despite coffee rust's impact on Southeast Asian production, global coffee prices did not rise because Brazil's expanding production compensated for the losses. Meanwhile, many parts of Africa also suffered from coffee rust, although impacts varied greatly. The presence of coffee rust in Asia and Africa constrained production, which fell behind that of the Americas (Clarence-Smith 2003). Latin America remained free from coffee rust until the 1970s; by that time, it had consolidated its position as the world's dominant coffee-producing region.

The War of a Thousand Days in Colombia

At the end of the nineteenth century, coffee prices plunged as excess production saturated the market. The War of a Thousand Days (1899–1903) in Colombia began as producers experienced falling coffee prices, and the government faced bankruptcy due to dropping income from coffee exports. Elite coffee planters, mainly members of the Liberal Party who argued for laissez-faire economic policies, went to war with the opposing Conservatives, as both sides aimed to dominate politics and set economic policies. The war resulted in 60,000–130,000 deaths, and destroyed or damaged many coffee plantations

(*Encyclopaedia Britannica Online* 2009). A bipartisan coalition emerged in the wake of the war and, despite ongoing tensions, steered Colombia toward economic development, infrastructural improvement, and political stability for the next three decades. Unfortunately, competing interests and resistance among the upper classes to addressing social problems laid the foundations for violence and social conflicts that have confounded Colombia since the mid twentieth century (Jiménez 1995b).

Coffee Prices, Social Injustice, and Civil War in Central America

The development of Central American nations has been intimately linked with the spread of coffee and coffee producers' activist roles in national politics. In the nineteenth century, Central American coffee emerged as a valuable commodity in European markets due to fine flavor, and attracted investors eager to make a profit. Large coffee producers in El Salvador, Guatemala, and Nicaragua became leading politicians and supported legislation in their favor. In each country, the implementation of liberal policies and associated laws allowed large coffee producers to expropriate land from indigenous people and coerce them to labor on coffee, sugar, and cotton plantations. In the process, indigenous cultures and traditions were undermined (McCreery 1995; Peckenham and Street 1985). The profound social inequities nourished a nascent resistance among indigenous peoples and rural poor that ultimately fueled Central America's civil wars of the 1970s and 1980s (Paige 1993; Williams 1994).

In El Salvador, falling coffee prices in the 1930s coincided with rising communist activity in the countryside. Indigenous peoples and poor mestizos who had been forced to labor on coffee plantations found themselves without work due to the economic crisis. Land scarcity, impoverishment, and perhaps hopes ignited by communist ideals, intersected with the economic crisis to trigger the rebellion of 1932. The El Salvadoran government, convinced of a communist conspiracy, sent the military to massacre thousands of indigenous people who were struggling to regain their land rights and improve their living conditions. The dominant classes believed that they were upholding civil order by quelling threats to the status quo from indigenous people and communists. As one scholar observed, "Actually, what they were doing by contributing to these sad and tragic events was mortgaging the democratic future of their country for years to come" (Pérez Brignoli 1995:256–257).

The Coffee Cycle and Brazil

By the late 1800s, Brazilian coffee represented two-thirds or more of global coffee production in every year. The growth in global coffee supply, led by Brazil, resulted in a 40 percent drop in coffee prices between 1875 and 1886.

The dropping prices meant that coffee became affordable for the general population. Coffee consumption increased steadily as more people adopted it. In the USA, coffee consumption increased 2,400 percent between 1783 and 1883, reflecting population growth as well as coffee's growing popularity. Even so, demand did not grow as quickly as supply, and low prices threatened producers' economic well-being. Producers hoped for Brazilian frosts to damage harvests and send prices up, as long as bad weather spared their own plantations. In 1887, a killing frost hit Brazil and sent prices higher, but plantations recuperated by the end of the century and prices collapsed. Twelve subsequent severe frosts occurred between 1904 and 1994. With each frost, prices rose and encouraged geographic diversification and increased production, which repeatedly cycled into more coffee supply and lower prices (Topik 2003).

Brazil's predominant presence on global coffee markets compelled it to take extraordinary steps to protect producers. It followed the policy of exporting the amount of coffee that global markets could absorb after the rest of the world's production was taken into account. This strategy helped to uphold world prices, but also encouraged other countries to expand production. Brazil's market share gradually fell as global production climbed. In the 1920s, coffee supplies vastly exceeded demand. The Brazilian government, anxious to shore up prices, disposed of tons of excess coffee by burning it or dumping it into the ocean. Within ten years, it destroyed the equivalent of two years of Brazilian coffee production (Daviron and Ponte 2005).

Ramifications of the Coffee Cycle

The coffee cycle has posed a constant challenge for the economic development of producing countries, even though the contexts of coffee supply and price volatility have been changing. As coffee's geographic expansion and global production have increased, dramatic drops in supply have become less likely, but risks of overproduction have increased. Many nations have designed policy initiatives to manage coffee production and mitigate market volatility. According to some studies, the political dimensions of managing coffee and disseminating information influence the coffee cycle as much as available supplies. Brazil has attempted to ameliorate price fluctuations by storing excess production and keeping the quantity in storage secret. Similarly, Colombia has endeavored to maintain uncertainty about the actual size of its harvest and stored amounts. From another perspective, the economic dimensions pale beside the suffering and enduring inequities associated with coffee production through its history of slavery, land expropriation, forced labor, and the disruption of rural livelihoods and indigenous cultures. It is fair to say that coffee has shaped the histories of nations, social inequality, and human rights around the world.

Questions for Reading, Reflection, and Debate

1. What is the coffee cycle, and why does it matter to coffee producers and consumers?
2. Why have Brazilian frosts had such a major impact on global prices?
3. Why do Brazil and Colombia think that price fluctuations will be reduced if they keep secret the size of their stored coffee supplies?
4. Given the relationships between coffee production and social tragedies, do you think it is possible to produce a commodity like coffee without economic problems or human suffering?
5. Besides coffee, what other major commodities experience price fluctuations? In comparison to coffee, do you think the reasons for price fluctuations of other commodities are similar or different?

16

EFFORTS TO MITIGATE THE COFFEE CYCLE AND THE DISTRIBUTION OF POWER

Countries that compete in the production of a primary good rarely cooperate to control production levels in order to uphold prices. However, for a time in the mid twentieth century, coffee-producing and -consuming countries signed international agreements that stabilized coffee prices and helped to mitigate the coffee cycle. Thus coffee became one of the first "regulated" commodities (Ponte 2002). Toward the end of the century, however, shifts in the geopolitical balance of power in conjunction with neoliberal economic policies and globalization processes undermined incentives for international coffee agreements. Indeed, processes of globalization have impacted the production and distribution of many goods. Today, clothing, computer components, electronics, and household goods are as likely to be manufactured in China, Mexico, India, or any number of countries, as in the USA. Profits increase if labor costs can be minimized; therefore TNCs move production and processing sites to regions where labor costs are low. Similarly, low labor costs result in cheaper coffee, but if coffee prices vary unpredictably, profits are also uncertain. By examining efforts to mitigate the coffee cycle within its historical context, it is possible to see how the distribution of power in coffee markets evolved during the twentieth century.

Initial Efforts to Mitigate the Coffee Cycle

Between 1906 and the late 1930s, Brazil produced the majority of the world's coffee and demonstrated the utility of price stabilization policies. It compelled merchant firms to sign cooperative agreements, stockpiled surplus production, and controlled export volumes, even at the cost of destroying excess production. By these policies, Brazil wrested power away from brokerage firms that had controlled exports, and became a leader in shaping international coffee markets.

World War II (1939–1945) changed global market dynamics. Europe's coffee imports practically ceased, and coffee prices collapsed. Anxious to protect its interests and shore up Latin American governments that depended on coffee exports for solvency and stability, the US government signed the Inter-American Coffee Agreement in 1940. The agreement raised coffee prices by 60 percent, until the USA entered the war in response to Pearl Harbor (December 7, 1941). At that time, the USA froze its coffee import prices, and effectively took control of the global coffee market as the dominant buyer. During and following the war, coffee markets became fragmented as Europe's imperial powers favored coffee from their own colonies and placed import taxes and quotas on other coffees. Through this period, most producing countries attempted to protect their coffee production by establishing state-run market boards and institutes to control domestic prices and regulate exports (Daviron and Ponte 2005). Lacking international coordination, global coffee exports exploded and prices dropped precipitously by the mid-1950s. In Latin America, producing countries negotiated the Mexico Agreement (1957) and the subsequent Latin American Agreement (1958) in hopes of stabilizing prices. These accords failed because African countries, which emerged as major producers following World War II, did not participate and their production continued to swamp global markets.

The Threat of Communism and the International Coffee Agreements

Low coffee prices in the 1950s coincided with the rise of the Cold War and fears in the USA of communist influence in Latin America. Military experts and political advisors expressed concerns that the low coffee prices could destabilize coffee-producing countries, perhaps leading to communist-controlled governments. European allies shared similar concerns, and consuming countries joined negotiations with producing countries to design an international accord to establish and enforce coffee-production quotas. By setting limits on global coffee production, consumers and producers alike hoped to benefit from more stable prices (and profits). The world's major coffee-consuming nations and most of the coffee-producing countries signed the first International Coffee Agreement (ICA) in 1962. In association with the ICA, the International Coffee Organization (ICO) formed as an intergovernmental body for addressing problems in the world coffee economy through international cooperation. Subsequent agreements were signed in 1968 (although the USA delayed), 1976, and 1983, which endured until 1989 (ICO 2009). General consensus exists that between 1962 and 1989, the ICAs proved largely successful to mitigate price volatility and stabilize global markets (Akiyama and Varangis 1990; Talbot 1997).

The ICAs worked because producing countries implemented policies to constrain production, and consuming countries cooperated by rejecting coffee that exceeded producers' quotas. Of course, producing countries attempted with each successive ICA to renegotiate for larger quotas. Some excess production certainly managed to be traded, in particular among countries that did not sign the ICAs. The ICO set an indicator price band; when prices fell below, quotas were tightened. When prices shot above the band, as when a severe frost hit Brazil in 1975, quotas were lifted until prices normalized. Under ICA regulations, the world avoided coffee crises, such as those triggered by excessive supplies in the late 1800s and 1950s. Moreover, the ICAs helped producing nations retain an important percentage of the profits from coffee. Small coffee producers in many parts of the world improved their living standards during this period, and many producing nations used the income from coffee exports to invest in infrastructural improvements and other development projects (Talbot 2004).

In 1989, efforts to negotiate a fifth ICA failed. Changes in global tastes had increased demand for arabica coffees, while demand for robusta (used mainly in instant coffee) had fallen. Negotiations failed to redistribute quotas accordingly among arabica- and robusta-producing countries, and this inflexibility frustrated roasters as well as arabica producers. Cooperation among coffee-producing countries fell apart with disagreements over quotas, free riding, and the problem of non-member consuming countries that purchased (and exported) over-quota coffee at reduced prices. The USA's overriding incentive to back ICAs evaporated as the Cold War dissipated peacefully under Gorbachev's policy of *perestroika* (restructuring) in the Soviet Union (Brown 2007; Love 1999). Meanwhile, coffee-roasting TNCs (such as Nestlé, Phillip Morris, Proctor & Gamble) had extended their control over the coffee commodity chain through the 1980s. The ICA constrained their efforts to further increase profits and market control; they lobbied against another ICA. The US government concluded that ICAs were no longer in its interest. US withdrawal ended the hopes for a renewed agreement.

The Post-ICA Era and the Coffee Crisis of 1999–2003

Within six months of the end of the quota system, control over producer stocks was transferred from public agencies to private trading companies, and stocks moved from producing countries to consuming countries. Producing countries lost most of their influence in international markets, and price stabilization programs and market boards faltered or went bankrupt (Daviron and Ponte 2005). With market deregulation and reorganization, international prices dropped. According to the ICO, the indicator price for coffee averaged $1.34 per pound in the last five years of the ICA (1984–1988). Over the first five years after the ICAs ended, the indicator price averaged 78 cents per pound (ICO 2009). During 1994, drought and a frost in Brazil sent the price up, but the harvests soon recovered. Without quotas to limit production, every country produced coffee at will. The 1989/1990 harvest, which was the last influenced by the quotas, amounted to 94 million bags of coffee. By the 1999/2000 harvest, production reached an incredible 130 million bags, well above predictions and far in excess of global demand of about 105 million bags (ICO 2009). Prices began a four-year freefall, reaching a 100-year low in real terms, and falling below the cost of production for many growers (Varangis *et al.* 2003).

Falling prices became an international crisis as coffee farmers were unable to repay loans, coffee laborers lost their jobs, and countries dependent on coffee exports found their budgets in arrears. Between 1999 and 2001, Central American countries experienced a 44 percent decline in revenue, and 540,000 people lost employment (Varangis *et al.* 2003). In El Salvador, malnutrition affected 45 percent of the children in coffee-growing households. In Papua New Guinea, where over half the population depends on coffee growing, employment on coffee estates fell by 40 percent; smallholders' daily income fell to $1 per day, and many could not pay their children's school fees. In Ethiopia, where 1.2 million people work in the coffee sector, malnutrition surged as families tried to survive on one meal a day; urban unemployment grew rapidly as coffee workers arrived to seek work, and the government suffered budgetary problems because half of its income depended on coffee exports. Globally, the crisis exacerbated poverty, social unrest, rural-to-urban migration, and production of illegal drugs (Osorio 2003).

Most coffee farmers had limited options to cope with the crisis, but because of the costs implied in removing a perennial crop such as coffee, few considered replacing plantations with another crop. Instead, farmers reduced their labor in coffee, abandoned their plantations to migrate in search of work, or diversified into other activities. One cross-national study of the crisis in Mexico, Guatemala, and Honduras (Eakin *et al.* 2006; Tucker *et al.* 2010) showed that farmers' perceptions and responses varied, even when they experienced similar price declines. Farmers in Mexico and Guatemala perceived the greatest hardship from the crisis; most of their land was planted in coffee and they had limited options to adopt new crops. Having benefited from government programs in the past, they were disappointed that the government failed to curb the crisis. They deeply felt their change of fortune. Honduran farmers in the study lived in a region where coffee had recently become an export crop. While they had fewer material goods than their Mexican and Guatemalan peers, they produced staples to feed themselves, had land to plant new crops, and had access to microcredit cooperatives. They did not expect government support. Comparatively few reported that low coffee prices represented a major problem. Thus farmers' perceptions of the crisis related to their level of dependence on coffee income, experience with government programs, and availability of land or other resources (such as microcredit) to diversify and compensate for low coffee prices. Unfortunately, few smallholder coffee farmers around the world had enough land or resources to adapt easily to the crisis.

The Conventional Commodity Chain and the Concentration of Power

Although oversupply contributed to the coffee crisis, multiple factors combined to create the crisis. In order to understand the changes that set off the crisis, it is helpful to consider the coffee commodity chain (Figure 16.1). A commodity chain is defined as "a network of labor and production processes that result in a finished commodity" (Hopkins and Wallerstein 1986 cited in Talbot 2002:703). At each link in the chain, actors have the opportunity to gain income. The total income from the commodity is distributed across each actor in the chain, and relative power in the market chain influences how much income is apportioned. Following the collapse of the ICAs in 1989, the producers' percentage of the total income from coffee fell steadily. Through the 1970s and 1980s, producing countries had retained 20 percent of the total income, while consuming countries controlled around 55 percent. By 1995, the proportion obtained by producing countries fell to 13 percent, and consuming countries gained 23 percent (Ponte 2001). By 2002, coffee farmers received about 2 percent of the cost of a cup of coffee sold in a coffee shop (Osorio 2002). The change in this distribution of income related to reorganization in the coffee commodity chain and associated corporate strategies.

In the first link of the conventional commodity chain, producers sell their beans to intermediaries, who may be local- or regional-level traders (often called "coyotes" in Latin America), cooperatives, agents, or regional processors. Or they may sell to exporters or market boards, depending on the country. The coffee may change hands several times before reaching exporters who sell it as green beans to international traders. Beginning in the 1980s, international traders, including importers and brokers, began to experience restructuring. Small and mid-sized traders found themselves unable to compete. They went out of business, merged to form larger firms, or were bought out by large trading companies. While the international trading market became more concentrated, coffee-roasting TNCs decided to outsource their supply management. Traders had to improve their supply networks to meet TNC demands, and therefore pursued vertical integration by moving into domestic trade and sometimes even to estate production, which is a way to move "upstream," or toward the producer, on the chain. By outsourcing, TNCs gained flexibility; they became less dependent on any given supplier or trader and reduced costs. By concentrating on marketing and branding, TNCs increased market control and their percentage of the total income, and capitalized on opportunities to create new products (Ponte 2001). As long as global coffee markets continue to produce excess volumes, TNCs will be free to pick and choose, and keep the prices they pay low.

TNCs and the Consolidation of Market Power

The curious thing is that most coffee consumers today barely notice price fluctuations. As recently as the 1970s, price changes in coffee markets were translated to consumers in higher or lower coffee prices. In 1976, when prices

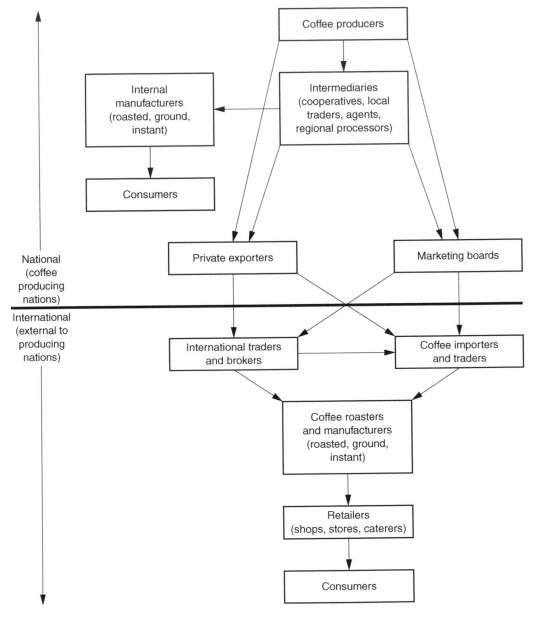

Figure 16.1 Conventional coffee commodity chain.

rose in the wake of a Brazilian frost, TNCs tried to mute consumer anger by resisting further price increases, shrinking the size of a can of coffee (16 ounces to 13 ounces) and recommending that smaller quantities of grounds be used to brew each cup. When prices fell again by 1980, TNCs did not return to the larger-sized can, and thus profits rose. They adapted this strategy successfully in subsequent moments of global price increases, by edging up prices and then neglecting to lower them. Thus the price that consumers spend for roasted and ground coffee became disconnected from global market prices (Talbot 1997). Today, advances in processing, roasting, and blending techniques permit coffee companies to maintain prices and similar coffee taste even when they add low-quality robustas to their blends. Thus they can pass off inferior coffee as high quality, and maintain or expand profits even if costs rise. TNCs typically seek the cheapest possible coffee to keep costs low. Now the costs of transporting, processing, and marketing in the conventional coffee chain cost more than the coffee itself.

Producing nations face a disadvantage. Since 1989, they have attempted repeatedly through the ICO to establish an effective price stabilization agreement. But they have been unable to counteract the market domination of TNCs without the support of consuming countries. The ICO has continued to operate, but it has not gained influence in global markets. Producers must accept the prices offered in the market, and face hardship when prices fall. The need for income creates the perverse incentive to continually increase production, even though producers realize that it may backfire should prices collapse. Farmers have told me that they hope for harvests to fail in other parts of the world to lift their prices. Some governments of coffee-producing countries offer limited support or protection for coffee producers, but international donor agencies to which many producing countries are indebted require free markets as part of their neoliberal policy prescriptions. As a result of technological, political, and economic changes, TNCs have increased profits, market control, and the ability to manage coffee supplies to their advantage. Producers have lost income, and consumers have lost quality in the TNC brands while paying higher prices. In order to redistribute power and income more equitably, TNCs' supplies would need to be threatened, as can happen when a killing frost hits Brazil, but such shocks tend to be temporary. TNCs' control over markets substantially reduces the possibility of better prices for producers in the long term. Realization of the inequities in global markets has contributed to the development and growing popularity of alternative trade arrangements.

Questions for Reading, Reflection, and Debate

1. What other products are subject to price fluctuations? Are there parallels in the reasons for price volatility for coffee and other commodities?

2. If the price of your favorite beverage doubled or tripled, would you change how much you drank it? If the price fell, would you drink more or the same amount? If everyone acts similarly, what do you think would happen at the national or international level if the prices were to change dramatically up, or down?

3. When TNCs choose to substitute higher-quality with lower-quality coffee, what may be the broader consequences? (Consider consumers, producers, and competitors.)

4. Imagine that you are a farmer who depends on coffee production for most of your annual income.

    - Under what circumstances would you be willing to reduce your coffee production? Why?
    - In the absence of incentives to reduce your production, would you choose to expand production, even knowing the risks of price volatility? Explain your answer.

17

A BRIEF HISTORY OF FAIR TRADE

When you go into a supermarket to buy coffee, you will find a dizzying array of choices, from traditional standards like Folgers and Maxwell House and instant coffees, to a range of specialty varieties that feature different roasts, decaffeination, and a few that carry "organic," "shade grown," or "bird friendly®" labels. Some of the coffees will carry a fair trade label, stamped in a prominent location. It's hard enough to choose among so many alternatives, but the fair trade option presents another challenge. Nearly everyone has an idea about the meaning of fair trade, yet few are really sure what it means or why it is different from free trade. Part of the confusion arises from the seemingly countless labels and organizations claiming to be fair trade, and differing information on how it works and what it accomplishes. By exploring the history and recent developments in fair trade markets, this chapter aims to clarify why fair trade emerged, how it evolved to encompass many different organizations and certifications, and the challenges it faces.

A Philosophy, a Movement, and a Network

Fair trade refers to an alternative marketing strategy that aims to mitigate the inequitable trade relationships that have come to characterize the world economic system. In general, proponents of fair trade share an underlying philosophy that economic relationships should work in favor of a more equitable and sustainable global society. Fair trade supporters aspire to reduce poverty, counteract unfair terms of trade, and contribute to social justice and human rights. The movement arising from this philosophical standpoint has a broad-based approach that dates back to the period following World War II (Fridell 2007). Everyone who supports fair trade actively or philosophically can be considered part of the fair trade movement.

The fair trade network refers to the non-government organizations, entrepreneurs, businesses, labeling initiatives, certification entities, producer organizations, and cooperatives that currently promote and participate in fair trade as a guiding principle of their work. The network is sometimes equated with the fair trade movement, but I distinguish them to better explain the historical development of fair trade. Growing within the fair trade movement, the fair trade network emerged in recent decades as businesses and organizations expanded their fair trade entrepreneurial efforts and began to build alliances toward common goals. The network is informal, having no centralized governance structure, but there are several umbrella organizations that businesses and organizations may choose to join. Fair trade organizations and businesses constitute a network in the sense that they ascribe to similar principles, which include offering fair prices, providing safe working conditions, encouraging environmentally sustainable practices, and supporting community development and democratic organization. Additionally, many fair trade organizations aspire to foster transparent and accountable relationships, respect cultural identity, and ensure children's rights (Fair Trade Federation 2007). Businesses committed to fair trade aim to fulfill these principles by building direct trade relationships. With direct trade, money that would have been paid to intermediaries goes to producers.

Origins of Fair Trade

The slogan "Trade not Aid" reflects the current philosophy of the major players involved in fair trade today. In its earliest days, however, the movement envisioned fundamental transformations in the global economy. Many early thinkers believed that changing the inequitable trade relationships required macrolevel (national and international) regulations and enforcement to ensure that nations of the global South would receive a larger portion of the profits for their primary products. This perspective emerged because politicians and scholars perceived that inequities in the global economy had contributed to World War II. Theorists reasoned that if developing countries could obtain a fairer price for their goods, it would facilitate stronger, more diverse, and versatile national economies. The Bretton Woods Accord in 1944 (Table 17.1) provided protections to support prices and stabilize developing countries' economies through modest constraints on free trade. This approach received further support with the Havana Charter, signed in 1948, which endeavored to regulate international trade through commodity controls to ensure reasonable prices. These agreements fostered import-substitution industrialization (ISI), an effort to facilitate industrial expansion in southern nations so they could capture greater profits by processing their primary products and selling the value-added goods. Under ISI efforts in the 1960s and 1970s, many countries expanded their industrial sectors, boosted employment, and began to reduce poverty (Fridell 2007). Nonetheless, fundamental inequities in the global market endured. Political efforts to motivate more equitable trade made some progress, but it proved difficult to enforce national policies and international agreements designed to support fairer trade arrangements. While higher-level efforts advanced slowly, individuals and small businesses began to build direct trade relationships with producers to offer fairer prices.

In the USA, fair trade practices can be traced to Edna Ruth Byler, an American businesswoman. During a visit to Puerto Rico in 1946, she saw women producing fine needlecrafts, and observed their impoverished conditions. She offered to take women's handmade lace to the USA. She sold the goods and returned the money directly to the artisans. Soon after, Byler founded the Overseas Needlepoint and Crafts Project (ONCP). She sold goods at the Mennonite World Conference in Switzerland in 1952; subsequently, the Mennonites decided to support the work. Across the next 30 years, she sold crafts produced by talented artisans living in developing countries, and tried to spread her convictions that direct trade relationships could mitigate poverty. The organization evolved into SELFHELP Crafts, and then became Ten Thousand Villages, a global fair trade organization with $20 million in annual sales (Ten Thousand Villages 2009).

Byler's efforts contributed to the early spread of alternative trade organizations (ATOs), part of a pattern in North America and Europe in which church groups and social justice organizations became key supporters of fair trade (Jaffee 2007). By the 1970s, ATOs in the USA started holding annual conferences to share information and cooperate toward meeting social justice goals. The growth in ATOs occurred in tandem with funding for ISI initiatives from international donor agencies, and the United Nations Conference on Trade and Development (UNCTAD) had some success encouraging industrialized nations to adopt regulatory mechanisms on trade. The 1970s represented a pinnacle of fair trade initiatives, because grassroots, governmental, and international mechanisms worked synergistically toward changing inequitable trade patterns (Fridell 2007). In this same period, however, governmental intervention in markets and international market regulations received increasing criticism as economic growth rates declined in northern nations. Pressure to deregulate markets began to reverse steps that had been taken toward fairer global trade, and dissolved the system created by the Bretton Woods Accord (Brenner and Theodore 2003). The USA in particular made political decisions that led to market deregulation, fostered increased foreign investment in Wall Street, and spurred the US trade deficit. These changes moved the global economy toward unregulated free trade and undermined ISI initiatives.

Fair Trade in Recent Times

Today, the political principles that support free trade, market deregulation, privatization of state-owned enterprises, and the free flow of capital are known

Table 17.1 Fair Trade Timeline

Year	Activity
1944	Bretton Woods Accord set principles to foster post-WWII free trade but provided options to developing countries' governments to protect their economies from exploitative international trade
1946	Edna Ruth Byler, volunteering with the Mennonite Central Committee, started selling handmade lace made by Puerto Rican women in the USA, and returning the money directly to the women
1948	Havana Charter encouraged international commodity-control arrangements to ensure reasonable commodity prices to foster stability in southern countries
1949	Sales Exchange for Refugee Rehabilitation and Vocation (SERRV) started supporting refugees from WWII
1952	The Overseas Needlepoint and Crafts Project, founded by Edna Ruth Byler, sold crafts at the Mennonite World Conference in Basel, Switzerland
1962	International Coffee Agreement was established to constrain overproduction and price volatility
1964	First United Nations Conference on Trade and Development (UNCTAD) started working toward fairer trade between northern and southern nations
1964	Oxfam Trading was formed, later became the fair trade branch of Oxfam International
1968	Overseas Needlepoint and Crafts Project became SELFHELP Crafts
1973	First fairly traded coffee imported to the Netherlands from Guatemala
1986	Equal Exchange formed to import fair trade coffee to the USA
1988	Solidaridad in the Netherlands established the first standardized criteria for fair trade and created the "Max Havelaar" label for its fair trade certified goods
1989	Fair trade labeling initiatives started spreading across Europe, North America, and Japan
1989	International Federation for Alternative Trade (IFAT) was founded as a global network of fair trade organizations

1989	The International Coffee Agreement (ICA) collapsed when the USA refused to negotiate new terms. The ICA's end gave new urgency for fair trade coffee initiatives
1992	The Fairtrade Foundation was founded in the United Kingdom with the support of many human-rights organizations (Christian Aid, Oxfam, Traidcraft, and the World Development Movement)
1994	Fairtrade Foundation, UK, launched Green & Black's Maya Gold Chocolate, Cafédirect Coffee, and Clipper Tea as fair trade brands
1994	North American Alternative Trade Organizations (NAATO) incorporated formally with an agreement among independent organizations that had been holding annual fair trade conferences since the 1970s
1995	NAATO changed its name to Fair Trade Federation
1996	SELFHELP Crafts changed its name to Ten Thousand Villages
1997	Fairtrade Labelling Organizations International (FLO) formed in Bonn, Germany, as an umbrella organization to unite fair trade organizations worldwide, harmonize the various certification standards, and coordinate certification. As of 2009, it had 24 members, including 19 labeling initiatives covering 23 countries
1997	Transfair Canada (an FLO affiliate) was founded
1999	Transfair USA (an FLO affiliate) was established and started certifying Fair Trade coffee
2000	IFAT reported that global fair trade sales exceeded $2.6 billion
2002	FLO created the Fairtrade certification mark[a]
2004	FLO divided into two organizations: FLO and FLO-CERT. FLO-CERT took on inspection and certification responsibilities. FLO retained responsibility to set its Fairtrade brand standards
2007	The three largest fair trade producer networks in the world joined FLO
2009	The Fair Trade Federation reached a membership of 270 organizations in the USA and Canada
2009	IFAT changed its name to the World Fair Trade Organization (WFTO)

Note

a The "Fairtrade" brand indicates certification by FLO standards, distinct from "fair trade" as used by alternative labels and in generic speech.

as neoliberal economics (Jessop 2002). While these principles have been associated with economic growth, they have also tended to disproportionately
benefit large companies and the wealthy, frequently with negative ramifications for poverty levels and economic stability (Nigh 1997). Despite free trade
rhetoric, northern countries have dominated trade agreements and maintained mechanisms for protecting certain sectors from external competition.
Developing countries have been compelled to eliminate protections and support for their industries and primary product sectors (agriculture, mining,
timber). If free trade were to function in reality as it does in theoretical
models, all nations would have similar access to markets, information, and
transportation, and abide by a common set of rules that prohibit protection-
ism. That is not the case.

The rise of neoliberal policies went hand in hand with an evolving political
atmosphere in North America and Europe that became unfriendly toward anything that could interfere with their free trade interests. The changes coincided with TNCs' growing power in global markets. Given the shift in the
political situation, ATOs chose to present themselves as compatible with free
trade. They moved away from the fair trade movement's original position that
governmental and international regulations should restrain the capitalist business interests. By emphasizing that direct trade relationships contributed to
the open flow of goods between the South and North, ATOs avoided the political opposition that might have arisen if they had spoken against free trade.
The slogan "Trade not Aid" differentiated ATOs from international development agencies, while fitting within the neoliberal philosophy (Jaffee 2007).

As global markets transitioned to neoliberal initiatives in the 1970s and
1980s, US consumers became increasingly anxious about the loss of family
farms and the possible environmental and health dangers of industrial agriculture with its dependence on chemical inputs. Interest in organic and locally
produced foods contributed to the founding of food cooperatives, and participants often shared interests in social justice as well as environmental sustainability. In 1986, a group of socially concerned consumers founded Equal
Exchange to import organic coffee at fair prices paid directly to producers.
Soon after, the Dutch non-government organization Solidaridad established
the first set of criteria to certify fair trade goods. A Mayan cooperative in
Mexico asked Solidaridad for help selling its coffee in Europe at fair prices. As
a result, Solidaridad started the Max Havelaar brand, adopting the name of a
character who struggled for social justice in a popular Dutch novel (Martínez-
Torres 2006). The Max Havelaar example inspired the spread of fair trade certification and labeling initiatives across Europe, the USA, Canada, and Japan.
The rapid proliferation of different fair trade criteria and competing brands
created problems for effective marketing, because customers encountered

competing and sometimes conflicting information. Today, there are two main umbrella networks: the World Fair Trade Organization (WFTO), and Fairtrade Labelling Organizations International (FLO).

World Fair Trade Organization

The WFTO began in 1989 as the International Fair Trade Association. Many fair trade organizations collaborated to create the organization and coordinate their efforts. It was the first umbrella organization that sought to unite organizations in the diffuse, informal fair trade network. Fair trade organizations in Europe, Africa, Asia, and Latin America coalesced into regional divisions. Globally, WFTO has incorporated over 350 member organizations that are committed to 100 percent fair trade. WFTO members represent all elements of the fair trade commodity chain, from producer cooperatives to regional networks to stores that sell fair trade goods. Members must agree to monitoring and regular inspections, show that they meet criteria, and attempt to follow fair trade principles in all dimensions of their business activities. WFTO members who sell fair trade coffee to consumers in northern nations guarantee that 100 percent of the content has been purchased at fair trade prices. Many prominent fair trade organizations in the USA and Canada are WFTO members, including Equal Exchange and Ten Thousand Villages. Only members may use the WFTO label.

The collapse of the ICA in 1989, followed by the implementations of the World Trade Organization in 1990 and the North American Free Trade Agreement in 1994, helped spread concern among ATOs for the effects on coffee growers. Coffee had already been privileged as the first agricultural fair trade commodity with the Equal Exchange and Max Havelaar brands. Through the 1990s, fair trade organizations continued to emerge and expand; many featured coffee. Social justice organizations in the United Kingdom created the Fairtrade Foundation in 1992, and began to sell fair trade coffee, chocolate, and tea. In 1994, a number of fair trade organizations in Canada and the USA coalesced as North American Alternative Trade Organizations, which subsequently became the Fair Trade Federation (FTO), encompassing 270 members in 2009. The Fair Trade Federation is a member of the WFTO.

Fairtrade Labelling Organizations International and FLO-CERT

FLO formed in 1997 to coordinate and harmonize the various criteria of its founding member organizations. FLO created the international "Fairtrade" mark to set FLO's members apart from other fair trade certified labels, and only its members can use it to show compliance with FLO principles. FLO affiliates Transfair Canada and Transfair USA were founded as national-level, third-party certifiers of fair trade enterprises in 1997 and 1999, respectively.

Transfair USA oversees producer organizations and businesses that follow the standards set by FLO. Producer organizations and businesses that receive certification from Transfair may use the Transfair fair trade label used in North America, which is different from the FLO Fairtrade label. The growth of fair trade and the need for unified certification procedures led to the division of FLO into two parts in 2004. FLO-CERT shouldered certification duties for producer and trade organizations in Africa, Asia, Latin America, and Europe. FLO-CERT has a network of independent inspectors in each region who are charged with monitoring and evaluating compliance with Fairtrade standards. FLO maintained the responsibilities to set its Fairtrade standards, support producers, and promote international fair trade. Today FLO encompasses 19 labeling organizations, three producer networks, and two associate members. While FLO and WFTO share fundamentally similar goals, they do not share members, and they use different labels. Unlike WFTO, FLO does not require members to commit to the principle of 100 percent fair trade.

Transnational Corporations Enter Fair Trade

The recent growth of fair trade relates to the popularity of the social justice goals, the perceived benefits of "Trade not Aid," and a more consistent message from fair trade marketing. In addition, knowledge of fair trade has been spreading. As recently as 2000, one Canadian researcher noted that employees at Starbucks were not sure what "fair trade coffee" meant, but that changed dramatically when Starbucks began to purchase a modest amount of fair trade coffee in 2002 (Fridell 2007). Starbucks' purchase of fair trade coffee points to a critical dimension in the recent expansion of fair trade: TNCs have been incorporating fair trade goods into their arsenal of products. In the case of Starbucks, fair trade supporters used a public campaign to pressure the company to purchase fair trade coffee. Other TNCs have chosen willingly to purchase fair trade goods, ostensibly to embrace social and environmental justice. They also use fair trade involvement to enhance their public image and take advantage of higher prices paid for fair trade products. TNCs can make a tremendous impact on the demand for fair trade goods, while making little change in their business practices. For example, Starbucks' purchases of fairly traded coffee represent only 2 percent of their total coffee acquisitions, but due to Starbucks' size, it doubled the volume of fair trade coffee sold globally.

TNC involvement has proven to be a double-edged sword. Although it has expanded the market for fair trade, it also has diluted the original message of fair trade and created conundrums for the movement. Whereas fair trade activists have aimed to increase equity and social justice by improving the terms of trade and income for producers of primary goods, TNCs focus on making profits by keeping costs as low as possible. The two goals are fundamentally contradictory. The original goal of fair trade businesses to offer an alternative to impersonal, profit-oriented trade practices has been confounded by the entrance of TNCs.

The process appears to involve cooptation. The Italian philosopher Antonio Gramsci observed that politically disadvantaged groups and dissidents can challenge the dominant ideas, or the hegemony, in a hierarchical society by introducing potentially revolutionary ideas and propositions (Forgasc 2000). When an idea becomes influential enough to threaten existing relationships, those in power may respond by assimilating the idea. The process typically involves subverting the idea in a way that ameliorates its threat, builds societal consensus, and recreates existing power relationships (Katz 2006). This is cooptation in the Gramscian sense, and through history the strategy has been a way for groups in power to deflect opposition. When cooptation fails or the governing groups cannot find a way to assimilate the idea, a counterhegemony may succeed in replacing the existing hegemony. Other possibilities also exist; groups in power may resort to overt coercion and violent oppression to eliminate counterhegemonic threats. Civil wars in Guatemala, El Salvador, and Nicaragua during the 1970s and 1980s escalated as entrenched social elites dismissed pressures to address their nations' profound inequities, and reacted to threats from militant reformists with violent military campaigns against segments of the general population. More broadly, groups in power resist challenges to their power by using overt and covert methods, and often a combination of both.

From a Gramscian perspective, the fair trade movement carried counterhegemonic ideas with the potential to threaten the global economic hegemony. TNCs muted its transformative potential by coopting the ideals of social justice through symbolic actions—buying small amounts of fair trade products in order to use a "fair trade" designation on certain products. ATOs became complicit in this cooptation by acceding to neoliberal political realities and welcoming TNCs' participation (although there were different opinions among fair trade supporters). At the same time, once TNCs decided to enter fair trade, ATOs could not have prevented it. TNC involvement highlights a central contradiction of fair trade: while aiming to alter the inequities of conventional markets, it depends on mechanisms of the same markets that generate those inequities (Jaffee 2007).

Companies can advertise coffee as fair trade as long as some of the beans come from fair trade sources. It is possible that good-intentioned employees of TNCs intend to transform their companies from within by encouraging purchases of fair trade goods. In some cases, TNCs may purchase fair trade, organic, and shade-grown coffee to address social justice concerns while also diversifying and strengthening their market shares. In other cases, however,

TNCs may be "blue-washing" themselves through nominal commitment to fair trade purchases. "Blue-washing" occurs when a business or program presents itself as socially and environmentally responsible without making any fundamental changes in its operations. By acquiring fair trade goods from a supplier, TNCs do not need to reform business practices in accordance with fair trade principles. Transfair USA audits fair trade transactions and certifies purchases that paid fair trade prices. Thus companies that work with Transfair can display the logo, yet their only commitment to fair trade is to purchase certified goods. Transfair does not make its audits public, so consumers cannot discover what percentage of a company's goods is fair trade.

While it is not clear that fair trade has transformed TNCs, it appears that TNCs are transforming fair trade. On one hand, TNC involvement has meant that fair trade cooperatives have been able to sell more of their products at fair trade prices; this is a major benefit, and a goal that fair trade supporters hoped to achieve by TNC involvement. On the other hand, TNC fair trade products now compete with the products of 100 percent fair trade businesses, which have fewer resources for advertising but a much greater commitment to support social and environmental sustainability through fair trade. Thus competition among different fair trade brands and the number of options facing consumers have been increasing. What does this mean for wise consumer decisions? Does fair trade really help people live better lives? The next chapter considers these challenging questions.

Questions for Reading, Reflection, and Debate

1. Have you seen fair trade labels where you shop? What kinds of items carry the labels? Do you buy them? Why or why not?
2. Do you agree that TNCs have coopted fair trade? Why or why not?
3. How did the rise of neoliberalism create challenges for ATOs? How did they respond? What other choices did they have?
4. What are the ethical puzzles and difficulties that have resulted as TNCs have become involved in fair trade?

18

CONUNDRUMS OF FAIR TRADE COFFEE
Building Equity or Reinventing Subjugation?

Fair trade has grown from its modest origins to become an influential alternative to conventional commodity chains. According to FLO, over 1.5 million farmers and workers in 58 developing countries participate in fair trade; if their families are included, the number of direct beneficiaries climbs to an estimated five million people. In 2008, FLO-certified sales exceeded $4 billion worldwide (FLO 2009). If all organizations involved with fair trade were included, the amount would be even greater; FLO does not represent all of them. When compared to the total value of global trade, which approached $25 trillion in 2007 (Miller *et al.* 2008), fair trade is barely a blip, but it is a rapidly growing segment of global trade.

Coffee was the first agricultural commodity to be sold as fair trade; therefore it may be the most familiar fair trade product. But fair trade and other specialty coffees carry a higher price than mainstream brands. Consumers may find it difficult to spend more on a bag of coffee unless it's clear that the additional cost provides something extra. If you choose to purchase fair trade coffee, are you making a difference in the lives of smallholder coffee producers?

Research on fair trade cooperatives around the world indicates that fair trade does provide benefits for coffee producers, but there are also challenges and drawbacks (Jaffee 2007; Sick 2008; Waridel 2002). Smallholder coffee producers who receive fair trade prices do better than their peers, especially when global coffee prices are low. During the coffee crisis of 1999–2003, fair trade coffee growers received a significantly higher income than those who did not sell their coffee as fair trade. Prices on the regular market fell as low as 45 cents per pound, too low to cover the costs of coffee production. Fair trade organizations paid $1.26–$1.41 per pound, depending on quality (Cycon 2005). Coffee farmers who received fair trade prices generally were able to cover their costs, maintain their plantations, and support their families, while others endured hardship (Bacon 2005; Osorio 2003; Varangis *et al.* 2003).

Challenges and Conundrums of Fair Trade

The situation facing fair trade farmers becomes more complicated when coffee prices rise above the minimum fair trade prices. According to FLO, fair trade coffee prices should at least meet the market price, and an additional 10 cents per pound must be added as a premium to invest in community development projects. But producer cooperatives need to lock in the price for their coffee before they sell it. Coffee prices move up and down continually, and prices may rise between the time a cooperative locks in the price and when the coffee is sold. If this happens, cooperatives may receive less than the best market price. Fair trade contracts can provide up to 60 percent of the purchase price to be advanced to producers, so they do not need to go into debt to hire coffee pickers and carry out maintenance prior to the harvest (Cycon 2005). This arrangement benefits farmers, but when the harvest comes, there is a delay between the sale and payment. The fair trade buyer may need to sell the coffee before paying the cooperative, which may also delay distribution of payments to producers. The delays inconvenience producers, especially when cooperatives have agreed to pay members only once or twice a year. Many farmers prefer to sell at least part of their harvest to intermediaries who pay immediately. A farmer may even be able to get a better price from the intermediaries if they offer a higher price than the price locked in with the fair trade buyer, which can happen in a year when prices increase above expectations. Fair trade contracts specify the quantity that must be provided by the cooperative. If a cooperative's members choose to sell their coffee elsewhere, due to the convenience or competitive prices, the cooperative may not be able to meet its quota (Camp *et al.* 2005). Defaulting on a contract can mean the end of a fair trade relationship; the fair trade purchaser may lose its investments of financial support, time, and travel, and the cooperative becomes known as an unreliable partner.

Since the end of the coffee crisis, prices have improved moderately, but many costs facing coffee farmers have risen. Costs of transportation, staple foods, education, health care, and labor have trended upward in most of the world, and conventional coffee farmers have also been subjected to climbing costs of fertilizer and other chemical inputs. In response to these circumstances, FLO increased the minimum ("floor") fair trade price by 5 cents per pound as of July 2008, while the 10-cent premium continued. Certified organic coffees received an additional 20 cents per pound above the floor price (FLO 2007).

In order to receive the fair trade price, producers must be members of a cooperative that has received fair trade certification. FLO contracts only with producer cooperatives, as part of the goal of supporting democratic organization. Moreover, it would be highly inefficient to make separate agreements with dozens of small producers. International trade ships goods in standardized 20- or 40-foot-long containers that carry up to 47,900 or 59,040 pounds, respectively. Fair trade businesses must contract with an entity large enough to fill a container, because shipping a partially filled container would increase the shipping cost per pound of coffee and drive up the price, as well as being an inefficient use of space. A small coffee producer may produce less than 1,000 pounds of coffee, so cooperatives of at least several dozen members or larger become the most viable partners for fair trade businesses.

TNCs, such as Starbucks, wish to extend fair trade certification to large producers. This would make it easier for TNCs to acquire "fair trade" coffee from fewer sources while continuing established contractual relationships. Large coffee producers can fill a container, but they represent a wealthy social class with alternative sources of income that does not need fair trade to make a living. Under pressure from TNCs, fair trade organizations are debating whether large producers should be eligible for fair trade certification (Jaffee 2007). It is not clear whether large producers would be required to pay fairer wages to their coffee pickers and employees, or if there would be any requirement for large producers to share the extra income with local communities. Without such requirements and monitoring, large producers would not have to fulfill the social sustainability principles of fair trade. Moreover, large producers typically raise sun-grown coffee and depend on heavy chemical inputs to maintain high production levels; it seems unlikely that they would be willing to change their production methods to become more environmentally sustainable. Another risk is that large producers would be able to outcompete small producers in the only niche in which small producers have a slight advantage. Because there is already an oversupply of coffee, letting large producers receive fair trade certification could reduce the chances for small producers to sell their coffee at fair trade prices. Fair trade could end up benefiting the wealthy more than the poor.

Costs of Certification

While fair trade can benefit smallholder coffee producers and their communities, it can also create new challenges. Certified fair trade farmers must abide by many rules to qualify for and maintain certification. Certification costs money and time, which cooperatives must bear unless they find a partner to defray the costs. For fair trade farmers seeking organic and shade-grown certification, the costs of following organic methods represent considerable demands on household and hired labor (Jaffee 2007). In particular, it takes a great deal of time and effort to make organic fertilizer and apply it individually to each plant several times a year. During my research in Honduras, I met with farmers who were in the process of being certified by Rainforest Alliance. They had to show that they had a certain number and variety of trees per hectare to meet biodiversity standards, and they had to place signs to label each building, including workers' dormitories, storage sheds, the family home, and the latrine. The signs lent an impersonal, odd appearance to the farms, as if they were no longer homes for families, but living museums created to entertain the certifiers. No one residing or working on the farms needed a sign to know the purpose of each building. Moreover, certifying criteria are subject to change. A colleague working in coffee-producing communities in southern Mexico informed me ruefully that she had encountered Mayan farmers' anger when they learned that to maintain their shade-grown certification they had to increase the number and diversity of trees in their plantations (H. Morales, personal communication, March 2008). The Mayan peoples' traditional coffee plantations have been recognized as some of the most biodiverse in Mexico, if not the world (Moguel and Toledo 1999). Farmers complained that since obtaining shade-grown certification, they had lost the freedom to decide how many and what kinds of trees they could plant on their lands. They resented the interference, knowing that an outside agent who did not understand their local ecological and climatic conditions could not determine the optimal number and combinations of trees for their plantations.

By contrast, businesses and consumers in coffee-importing nations can buy fair trade coffee without having to meet any standards. Fair trade businesses partnering with producers are supposed to follow principles of democratic organization, fair treatment of employees, and sustainable use of resources. While many local cooperatives and fair trade businesses in consuming countries attempt to fulfill these goals, no monitoring system verifies how well the principles are followed. Often, much of the cost and effort to obtain certification and maintain it must be borne by producers, not partner organizations and companies based in the North. Thus the expectations and costs placed on producers through the certification process may be viewed as yet another form of inequity.

Perhaps most troubling for fair trade producers is that more fair trade coffee is being produced than the market demands. Most cooperatives find it difficult to sell all of their coffee at fair trade prices. By some estimates, only 20 percent of the coffee produced by fair trade cooperatives is actually sold as fair trade. Farmers sell the rest at market prices (Cycon 2005). For fair trade producers who have also invested in obtaining organic or shade-grown certification, the difference between what they can sell at fair trade prices and at market prices usually represents a loss (although intermediaries may pay a better market price for organic than conventional coffee). To keep certification, farmers must maintain their whole plantation organically, even if they must sell part of their coffee to the conventional market.

Thus farmers may benefit from participating in fair trade, but it also poses risks and conundrums for them. Some fair trade cooperatives have been unable to make a profit, and have found the system to be impersonal and excessively demanding (Smith 2007). In some ways, fair trade has become a servant of the global system. Fair trade certification has required farmers to meet environmental and social standards set by people who live in distant lands. After the effort of gaining fair trade certification, farmers may not be able to get the best possible price for their products. Fair trade businesses, which ideally would offer even better payment arrangements, have constraints because they must work within global shipping, transportation, banking, and marketing systems that have evolved to meet the needs of large, profit-oriented businesses. Clearly, fair trade has yet to be truly fair, but it is not for lack of trying. Many producers, businesses, and consumers have a genuine commitment to fair trade as a means to work toward a more just, equitable, and sustainable world, even though they face great odds in a global system that functions to make profits.

For people who believe that the world can become a fairer and more equitable place, the failures of fair trade can be an incentive to motivate action rather than apathy. If fair trade has shortcomings, then how can it be made better? Consumers who purchase fair trade coffee, especially if it is 100 percent fair trade, can be assured that their choice does more to help smallholder coffee producers make a living than buying a major market brand. We surely will not make a difference by giving up and making do with the dull canned grounds that TNCs tried to pass off as good coffee before competition from specialty, organic, shade-grown, and fair trade coffee providers. In a way, the assessment of fair trade depends on the question asked. If the question is "Does fair trade consistently fulfill all of its objectives?" then it is not surprising that fair trade has shortcomings. Fair trade and all alternative trade arrangements are subject to standards and procedures established by a global system that resists equitable relationships by its very structures. But if the question is "Does fair trade generally provide a better income for producers than conventional markets?" the answer appears to be a cautious "yes," especially when incomes are assessed over an extended period.

We do not live in an ideal world; we live in a world that is constantly experiencing change. In every decision and action that we make, we have an opportunity to influence the direction that change will take. It may be difficult to believe, but choosing to buy coffee or other fair trade products from a 100 percent fair trade company can be more than a symbolic action. Supporting businesses that follow the fundamental principles of fair trade can be a way to foster community and sustainability where you live. Fair trade business means more than paying a better price to coffee producers; it can also mean paying employees better than minimum wage, reducing and recycling waste, making wise energy decisions, and working locally to address poverty and other social problems. Individuals can support equity, and social and environmental sustainability, by becoming involved in local organizations with a commitment to these principles. Drinking fair trade coffee can be a way to remember that we are connected intimately to people with whom we share this planet. With every sip, we inhale the essences of the air, rain, sun, and soil that nourished the coffee plants. We benefit from the care, sweat, and toil that brought the coffee to our table, and we know that we have made at least a small effort to respect the labor. Through coffee, we share a bond, and through our actions, we build a common fate.

Questions for Reading, Reflection, and Debate

1. How does fair trade certification (and other certification programs) create new challenges or risks for producers?
2. What risks or uncertainties do consumers encounter when purchasing fair trade goods? What differences may exist between goods with "fair trade" labels?
3. How are economic downturns and depressions likely to impact fair trade purchases for consumers? What would be the implications for producers?
4. How could fair trade be made to work more fairly? Should consumers and businesses in consuming countries be expected to meet certain standards to purchase or sell fair trade goods? Why or why not?

APPENDIX
A COFFEE CULTURE TIMELINE

~900	Rhazes (~852–932), an Arab physician, writes about *bunn*, which may have been coffee
~1000	Avicenna (~980–1037), eminent Arab philosopher, describes *bunn* in his Canon of Medicine
~1450	Coffee known in Yemen (no reliable historical record documents the arrival)
~1480	Sufi religious faithful drink coffee to stay awake through late-night devotions
~1500	Coffeehouses open in Mecca and Cairo
1511	Kha'ir Beg, Mecca's chief of police, bans coffee and coffeehouses
1511	The sultan of Cairo reverses Beg's ban on coffee
1521	Cairo experiences conflicts between coffeehouse customers and neighboring households angered at the late-night carousing
1536	Ottoman Turks occupy Yemen; take control of coffee production and trade through the port of Mocha
1537	Oromo warriors invade Ethiopia, and war interferes with coffee production and trade, allowing Yemen to become the major producer and exporter
1555	First coffeehouse opens in Constantinople
~1580	Murat III, sultan of Constantinople, bans coffee and closes coffeehouses, which proves only temporary
~1600	Pope Clement VIII purportedly baptizes coffee for Christian use
1600	The British East India Company is chartered
1602	The Dutch East India Company is chartered
1616	Dutchman smuggles a living coffee tree from Aden (Yemen) to Holland
1624	First record of coffee beans in Venice (some sources give 1638)
1633	The vizier of Constantinople, Murat IV, razes coffeehouses and punishes coffeehouse customers and owners by tying them in bags and throwing them into the Bosphorus
1640	First record of commercial coffee sales in Holland

~1650	Coffee beans reach Germany by way of Holland
1650	Oxford's first coffeehouse opens (some sources differ)
1652	London's first coffeehouse opens
1657	Coffee appears on apothecary lists in Germany
1658	The Dutch plant coffee in Ceylon (from seeds of the coffee tree smuggled from Aden to Holland)
1663	Regularly scheduled shipments of coffee to Holland from Yemen begin
1664	King Louis XIV's purported first taste of coffee
~1665	The first Dutch coffeehouse opens in The Hague
1668	Earliest known record of coffee in the New World
1669	Mohammad IV, sultan of Turkey, sends his ambassador Suleiman Aga to Paris; Aga entertains the French aristocracy with opulent coffee parties
1671	Marseilles' first coffeehouse opens
1672	Coffee sells commercially during a street fair on the outskirts of Paris
1674	"Women's petition against coffee" published in London; men reply in favor of coffee
1675	Charles II of England proclaims a ban on coffee and coffeehouses as "seminaries of sedition"; it is revoked before it takes effect due to public outcry
1679	Hamburg's first coffeehouse opens to serve British sailors and merchants
1683	Venice's first coffeehouse, The Blue Bottle, opens
1683	Italy's first coffeehouse opens (possibly earlier, but records are unreliable)
1688–1699	The Dutch introduce coffee to Java
1689	François Procope opens the Café Procope in Paris
1689	Boston's first coffeehouse opens
1700	London has 2,000 coffeehouses
1700	Philadelphia's first coffeehouse opens
1706	A coffee plant and seeds from Java arrive in the botanical gardens of Amsterdam
1711	Britain raises import duties on coffee
1714	Louis XIV receives a coffee plant from the burgomaster of Amsterdam; it is transplanted successfully to the botanical garden in Paris
1715–1717	French introduce coffee to the Caribbean (Hispaniola)
1718	Dutch introduce coffee to Surinam
~1720	Gabriel de Clieu smuggles a coffee seedling to Martinique

1721	Berlin's first coffeehouse opens
1724	Britain raises import duties on coffee
1727	Coffee is planted in Pará, Brazil
1730	British plant coffee in Jamaica
1732	Bach writes the Coffee Cantata in Germany
1738–1745	The War of Jenkins's Ear disrupts coffee shipments to Great Britain
1763	Venice has over 200 coffee shops
1775	Events culminating in the Boston Tea Party compel American patriots to forgo tea and embrace coffee
1777	Frederick the Great of Germany issues a manifesto promoting beer over coffee
1781	Frederick the Great bans coffee roasting except by wealthy Germans granted his permission
1790	The first wholesale coffee-roasting company and the first newspaper advertisement featuring coffee appear in the USA
1791–1803	A slave insurrection in St. Domingue (Haiti) causes a fall in coffee production, gives opening for profitable Brazilian expansion
1822	The first prototype of the modern espresso machine is invented in France
1840	The steam engine (developed by James Watt in 1765) is adapted to ocean-going vessels, which revolutionizes global shipping and facilitates coffee production in Central America
1850	Brazilian coffee production amounts to five times that produced in the rest of the world
1875–1886	World coffee prices fall 40 percent as production rises
1876	Coffee rust disease decimates large coffee plantations in Southeast Asia
1887	A killing frost hits Brazil's coffee plantations
1887	Brazil establishes its first experimental station for coffee research
1898	Global oversupply triggers falling coffee prices
1899–1902	War of a Thousand Days destroys coffee plantations in Colombia
1900	Invention of vacuum packing and long-term storage of ground coffee
1906	Invention of the first process for making instant coffee
1906	Brazil produces a record 82 percent of the world's coffee production
1906	The first commercial espresso machine is manufactured in Italy
1908	Frau Melitta Benz invents filter brewing in Germany
1927	The National Federation of Coffee Growers of Colombia forms
1935	Packaged, ground coffee amounts to 90 percent of US coffee sold

1959	An accord to limit production is signed among many producing countries including France and Portugal
1960	The Brazilian Coffee Institute promotes domestically owned instant coffee factories
1960	Colcafé, a Colombian coffee roaster, opens a domestic instant coffee factory
1962	The first ICA is signed jointly by consuming and producing countries.
1963	Creation of the ICO
1968	The second ICA goes into effect, but the US Congress holds up confirmation
1971	Starbucks opens as an independent coffee roaster in Seattle, Washington
1972	The 1968 ICA is not renewed
1974	USSR opens an instant coffee factory, stops instant coffee imports from Brazil
1975	Severe frost damages Brazil's coffee plantations as the harvest is ending; almost half of plantations require replanting
1976	A third ICA is signed
1980s	Philip Morris becomes the world's largest coffee company
1980	A fourth ICA is signed
1981	The National Federation of Coffee Growers of Colombia introduces the Juan Valdez logo
1987	Howard Schultz buys out Starbucks and starts opening coffee shops by that name
1989	Collapse of the ICA; world coffee prices fall with the elimination of quotas
1990	Vietnam emerges as a producer of robusta coffee
1993	Russia renews imports of instant coffee from Brazil
1994	A frost in Brazil causes prices to rise
1999	Vietnam becomes the world's second-largest coffee producer, pushing Colombia to third place
1999	Coffee crisis of 1999–2003 begins as supply grows and demand stagnates
2000–2001	World coffee prices fall to 100-year lows in real terms
2003	Coffee prices experience a slight recovery
2009	Starbucks has more than 15,000 coffee shops in over 50 countries

REFERENCES

Abramovitz, M. 2002. Wake Up and Smell the Caffeine. *Current Health 2* 28(5):28–31.

Akiyama, T. and P.N. Varangis. 1990. The Impact of the International Coffee Agreement on Producing Countries. *The World Bank Economic Review* 4(2):157–173.

Alcorn, J. 1990. Indigenous Agroforestry Strategies Meeting Farmer's Needs. In *Alternatives to Deforestation: Steps toward Sustainable Use of the Amazon Rain Forest*, ed. A. Anderson, 141–151. New York: Columbia University Press.

Allen, S.L. 1999. *The Devil's Cup: A History of the World According to Coffee*. New York: Ballantine.

Bacon, C. 2005. Confronting the Coffee Crisis: Can Fair Trade, Organic, and Specialty Coffees Reduce Small-Scale Farmer Vulnerability in Northern Nicaragua? *World Development* 33(3):497–511.

Baker, J.A., S.E. McCann, M.E. Reid, S. Nowell, G. Bechler, and K.B. Moyisch. 2005. Associations between Black Tea and Coffee Consumption and Risk of Lung Cancer among Current and Former Smokers. *Nutrition and Cancer* 52:15–21.

Bates, R.H. 1997. *Open-Economy Politics: The Political Economy of the World Coffee Trade*. Princeton, NJ: Princeton University Press.

Bayer Crop Science. 2010. *Di-Syston 15% Granular Systemic Pesticide: For Effective Systemic Protection of Coffee Trees in Puerto Rico and Fir Grown for Christmas Trees*. Online: www.bayercropscienceus.com/products_and_seeds/insecticides/di-syston.html (accessed July 25, 2010).

Belasco, W. 2002. Food Matters: Perspectives on an Emerging Field. In *Food Nations: Selling Taste in Consumer Societies*, ed. W. Belasco and P. Scranton, 2–23. New York: Routledge.

Beverage Marketing Corporation. 2009. *2009 Global Multiple Beverage Marketplace*. New York: Beverage Marketing Corporation.

Beyer, R. 2007. *The Greatest Presidential Stories Never Told: 100 Tales from History to Astonish, Bewilder and Stupefy*. New York: Collins.

Bourdieu, P. 1984 [1979]. *Distinction: A Social Critique of the Judgement of Taste*. Cambridge, MA: Harvard University Press.

Brando, C.H.J. 2009. Harvesting and Green Coffee Processing. In *Coffee: Growing, Processing, Sustainable Production—A Guidebook for Growers, Processors, Traders and Researchers*, 2nd rev. edn, ed. J.N. Wintgens, 610–740. Weinheim, Germany: Wiley-VCH Verlag.

Brenner, N. and N. Theodore. 2003. *Spaces of Neoliberalism: Urban Restructuring in North America and Western Europe*. Malden, MA: Wiley-Blackwell.

Brown, A. 2007. Perestroika and the End of the Cold War. *Cold War History* 7(1):1–17.

Brundtland Commission (World Commission on Environment and Development). 1987. *Our Common Future, Chapter 2: Towards Sustainable Development*. Online: www.un-documents.net/ocf-02.htm (accessed September 15, 2009).

Bryant, C.A., K.M. DeWalt, A. Courtney, and J. Schwartz. 2003. *The Cultural Feast: An Introduction to Food and Society.* Belmont, CA: Thomson Wadsworth.

Buchholz, D. 2002. *Heal Your Headache.* New York: Workman Publishing.

Camp, M., S. Flynn, A. Portalewska, and T.T. Cullen. 2005. A Cup of Truth. *Cultural Survival Quarterly* 29:17–25.

Campbell, G. 2003. The Origins and Development of Coffee Production in Réunion and Madagascar, 1711–1972. In *The Global Coffee Economy in Africa, Asia, and Latin America, 1500–1989,* ed. W.G. Clarence-Smith and S. Topik, 67–99. Cambridge: Cambridge University Press.

Campos, H. and A. Baylin. 2007. Coffee Consumption and Risk of Type 2 Diabetes and Heart Disease. *Nutrition Reviews* 65:173–179.

Carpenter, S. 2003. Bitter News for Tender Tongues. *Science* 299:1306.

Clarence-Smith, W.G. 2003. The Coffee Crisis in Asia, Africa, and the Pacific, 1870–1914. In *The Global Coffee Economy in Africa, Asia, and Latin America, 1500–1989,* ed. W.G. Clarence-Smith and S. Topik, 100–119. Cambridge: Cambridge University Press.

Clarence-Smith, W.G. and S. Topik. 2003. *The Global Coffee Economy in Africa, Asia, and Latin America 1500–1989.* Cambridge: Cambridge University Press.

Clark, D. 2004. The Raw and the Rotten: Punk Cuisine. *Ethnology* 43:19–31.

Clark, G., M. Huberman, and P.H. Lindert. 1995. A British Food Puzzle, 1770–1850. *The Economic History Review* 48(2):215–237.

Clark, T. 2007. *Starbucked: A Double Tall Tale of Caffeine, Commerce, and Culture.* New York: Little, Brown, and Company.

Clarkson, J. and T. Gloning, eds. 2003. *The Women's Petition against Coffee* (London 1674). Online: www.uni-giessen.de/gloning/tx/wom-pet.htm (accessed September 11, 2009).

Clarkson, J. and T. Gloning, eds. 2005. *The Mens Answer to the Womens Petition against Coffee* (London 1674). Online: www.uni-giessen.de/gloning/tx/mens-answer-1674.htm (accessed September 11, 2009).

Coffee Futures Trader. 2007. Coffee Futures: An Historical Perspective. Online: http://coffee-trader.blogspot.com/2007/10/coffee-futures-historical-perspective.html (accessed January 6, 2010).

Coffee Research Institute. 2006. *Coffee Consumption Statistics in the United States.* Online: www.coffeeresearch.org/market/usa.htm (accessed February 19, 2009).

Coffee Statistics Online. 2010. *Coffee Statistics Report 2010.* Online: www.coffee-statistics.com/coffee_statistics_ebook.html (accessed July 18, 2010).

Cohen, L.H. 1997. *Glass, Paper, Beans: Revelations on the Nature and Value of Ordinary Things.* New York: Doubleday.

Connery, B.A. 1997. IMHO: Authority and Egalitarian Rhetoric in the Virtual Coffeehouse. In *Internet Culture,* ed. D. Porter, 161–179. New York: Routledge.

Consumers International. 2005. *From Bean to Cup: How Consumer Choice Impacts Coffee Producers and the Environment.* London: Consumers International. Online: www.consumersinternational.org/Shared_ASP_Files/UploadedFiles/FDB0EF2D-14FE-4558-B219-A7FD81E089FB_CIcoffeereport.pdf (accessed January 8, 2010).

Curtis, K.R. 2003. Smaller is Better: A Consensus of Peasants and Bureaucrats in Colonial Tanganyika. In *The Global Coffee Economy in Africa, Asia, and Latin America, 1500–1989,* ed. W.G. Clarence-Smith and S. Topik, 312–334. Cambridge: Cambridge University Press.

Cycon, D. 2005. Confessions of a Fair Trader. *Cultural Survival Quarterly* 29:26–30.

Cycon, D. 2007. *Javatrekker: Dispatches from the World of Fair Trade Coffee.* White River Junction, VT: Chelsea Green Publishing.

Damodaran, A. 2002. Conflict of Trade-Facilitating Environmental Regulations with Biodiversity Concerns: The Case of Coffee-Farming Units in India. *World Development* 30:1123–1135.

Daviron, B. and S. Ponte. 2005. *The Coffee Paradox: Global Markets, Commodity Trade and the Elusive Promise of Development.* London and New York: Zed Books.

Descroix, F. and J.N. Wintgens. 2009. Establishing a Coffee Plantation. In *Coffee: Growing, Processing, Sustainable Production: A Guidebook for Growers, Processors, Traders, and Researchers,* 2nd rev. edn, ed. J.N. Wintgens, 182–249. Weinheim, Germany: Wiley-VCH Verlag.

Dicum, G. and N. Luttinger. 1999. *The Coffee Book: Anatomy of an Industry from Crop to the Last Drop.* New York: New Press.

Eakin, H., C. Tucker, and E. Castellanos. 2006. Responding to the Coffee Crisis: A Pilot Study of Farmers' Adaptations in Mexico, Guatemala and Honduras. *The Geographical Journal* 172(2):156–171.

Ellis, M. 2004. *The Coffee House: A Cultural History.* London: Weidenfeld & Nicolson.

Encyclopaedia Britannica Online. 2009. *The War of a Thousand Days.* Online: www.britannica.com/EBchecked/topic/593531/The-War-of-a-Thousand-Days (accessed December 31, 2009).

Encyclopaedia Britannica Online. 2010. *Kola Nut.* Online: www.britannica.com/EBchecked/topic/321308/kola-nut (accessed July 16, 2010).

EPA (United States Environmental Protection Agency). 2008. *Diazinon: Phase Out of all Residential Uses of the Insecticide.* Online: www.epa.gov/pesticides/factsheets/chemicals/diazinon-factsheet.htm (accessed July 25, 2010).

Eskes, A.B. and T. Leroy. 2009. Coffee Selection and Breeding. In *Coffee: Growing, Processing, Sustainable Production: A Guidebook for Growers, Processors, Traders, and Researchers,* 2nd rev. edn, ed. J.N. Wintgens, 61–90. Weinheim, Germany: Wiley-VCH Verlag.

Esposito, F., F. Morisco, V. Verde, A. Ritieni, A. Alezio, N. Caporaso, and V. Fogliano. 2003. Moderate Coffee Consumption Increases Plasma Glutathione but Not Homocysteine in Healthy Subjects. *Alimentary Pharmacology & Therapeutics* 17:595.

ETC Group. 2008. *Who Owns Nature? Corporate Power and the Final Frontier in the Commodification of Life.* Communiqué Issue #100. Ottawa: ETC Group.

Fair Trade Federation. 2007. *Principles for the Fair Trade Federation Members.* Online: www.fairtradefederation.org/ht/d/sp/i/8447/pid/8447 (accessed August 15, 2009).

Faris, S. 2007. *Starbucks vs. Ethiopia.* Online: http://money.cnn.com/magazines/fortune/fortune_archive/2007/03/05/8401343/index.htm (accessed January 8, 2010).

Farrell, J.J. 2006. Cup of Coffee. *Clergy Journal* 82(9):22.

Fernando, M.R. 2003. Coffee Cultivation in Java, 1830–1917. In *The Global Coffee Economy in Africa, Asia, and Latin America, 1500–1989,* ed. W.G. Clarence-Smith and S. Topik, 157–190. Cambridge: Cambridge University Press.

Ferraro, G. 2006. *Cultural Anthropology: An Applied Perspective,* 6th edn. Belmont, CA: Thomson-Wadsworth.

Flatto, E. 1990. Coffee Drinking and Sexual Desire. *Nutrition Health Review: The Consumer's Medical Journal* Fall 90(56):18.

Fletcher, A. 2006. *Healthy Soft Drinks Drive Global Beverage Growth.* Online: www.foodnavigator.com/Financial-Industry/Healthy-soft-drinks-drive-global-beverage-growth (accessed July 15, 2010).

FLO (Fairtrade Labelling Organizations International). 2007. *FLO International Adjusts Fairtrade Minimum Prices for Arabica Coffee to Cover Costs of Sustainable Production.* Online: www.fairtrade.net/index.php?id=721&type=123&cHash=4805201a6d&tx_ttnews[backPid]=614&tx_ttnews[pointer]=4&tx_ttnews[tt_news]=32 (accessed August 31, 2009).

FLO (Fairtrade Labelling Organizations International). 2009. *Facts and Figures.* Online: www.fairtrade.net/facts_and_figures.html (accessed August 29, 2009).

FMC Corporation. 2009. *Furadon Facts.* Online: www.furadanfacts.com (accessed July 25, 2010).

FNCC (National Federation of Coffee Growers of Colombia). 2009. *Colombian Coffee History.* Online: www.juanvaldez.com/menu/history/index.html (accessed December 14, 2009).

Food&Drinkeurope.com. 2003. *Competition Set to Increase in Global Drinks Market.* Online: www.foodanddrinkeurope.com/content/view/print/98656 (accessed July 26, 2010).

Forgasc, D., ed. 2000. *The Gramsci Reader: Selected Writings, 1916–1935.* New York: New York University Press.

Foster, R.J. 2008. *Coca-Globalization: Following Soft Drinks from New York to New Guinea.* New York: Palgrave Macmillan.

Foucault, M. 1995. *Discipline and Punish: The Birth of the Prison*, 2nd edn, trans. A. Sheridan. New York: Random House.

Fridell, G. 2007. *Fair Trade Coffee: The Prospects and Pitfalls of Market-Driven Social Justice.* Toronto: University of Toronto Press.

Funderburg, E. 2001. *Why Are Nitrogen Prices So High?* Online: www.noble.org/ag/soils/nitrogenprices/index.htm (accessed July 19, 2010).

Furtado, C. 1976. *Economic Development of Latin America: Historical Background and Contemporary Problems*, 2nd edn. Cambridge: Cambridge University Press.

Future Trends. 2001. *The Future of the Coffee Industry.* Online: www.globalchange.com/futurecoffee.htm (accessed July 26, 2010).

Gardner, C., B. Bruce, and G.A. Spiller. 1998. Coffee, Caffeine and Serum Cholesterol. In *Caffeine*, ed. G.A. Spiller, 301–324. Boca Raton, FL: CRC Press.

George, S.E., K. Ramalakshmi, and L.J.M. Rao. 2008. A Perception on Health Benefits of Coffee. *Critical Reviews in Food Science and Nutrition* 48(5):464–486.

Greenberg, R. 2010. *Cafe Ole! 5 Unique Coffee Traditions from around the Globe.* Online: www.nileguide.com/blog/2010/06/03/cafe-ole-5-unique-coffee-traditions-from-around-the-globe (accessed July 17, 2010).

Griffin, L.R. 2008. The Caffeine Advantage. *Men's Health* 23(2):102–104.

Gudmundson, L. 1995. Peasant, Farmer, Proletarian: Class Formation in a Smallholder Coffee Economy—1850–1950. In *Coffee, Society and Power in Latin America*, ed. W. Roseberry, L. Gudmundson, and M. Samper Kutschbach, 112–150. Baltimore, MD: Johns Hopkins University Press.

Gunder Frank, A. 1966. The Development of Underdevelopment. *Monthly Review* 18(4):17–31.

Harrison, K. 2006. *Carbofuran, Furadan, Curater.* Online: www.3dchem.com/moremolecules.asp?ID=263&othername=Furadan (accessed July 25, 2010).

Harvard Health Publications. 2004. Coffee: For Most It's Safe. *Harvard Women's Health Watch* 12(1):2–4.

Hattox, R.S. 1985. *Coffee and Coffeehouses: The Origins of a Social Beverage in the Medieval Near East.* Seattle: University of Washington Press.

Helman, C. 2010. *The World's Biggest Oil Reserves.* Online: www.forbes.com/2010/01/21/biggest-oil-fields-business-energy-oil-fields.html (accessed July 26, 2010).

Henrici, C.F. *c*.1734. *Libretto for J.S. Bach's Coffee Cantata.* Trans. unknown. Online: www.afactor.net/kitchen/coffee/kaffeeKantate.html (accessed September 5, 2009).

Higdon, J.V. and B. Frei. 2006. Coffee and Health: A Review of Recent Human Research. *Critical Reviews in Food Science and Nutrition* 46:101–123.

Hinrichs, R., N. Hunzelmann, A. Ritzkowsky, T.M. Zollner, T. Kerieg, and K. Scharffetter-Kochanek. 2002. Caffeine Hypersensitivity. *AllergyNet* 57:859.

Holmes, H. 2004. *Coffee Shop.* San Antonio, TX: U.S. Small Business Administration.

Homan, D.J. and S. Mobarhan. 2006. Coffee: Good, Bad, or Just Fun? A Critical Review of Coffee's Effects on Liver Enzymes. *Nutrition Reviews* 64:43–46.

Hopkins, T. and I. Wallerstein. 1986. Commodity Chains in the World Economy. *Review* 10(1):157–170.

Hopley, C. 2006. British Textiles Clothe the World. *British Heritage* 27(4):28–33.

ICO (International Coffee Organization). 2009. *Historical Data.* London: ICO. Online: www.ico.org/new_historical.asp (accessed January 6, 2010).

ICO (International Coffee Organization). 2010. *Letter from the Executive Director: Coffee Market Report June 2010.* Online: http://dev.ico.org/documents/cmr-0610-e.pdf (accessed July 18, 2010).

IHCAFE (Instituto Hondureño del Café) 2001. *Manual de Caficultura.* Tegucigalpa, Honduras: IHCAFE.

Iijima, M. 2010. *Travel Postcard: 48 Hours in Banda Aceh, Indonesia.* Online: www.reuters.com/article/idUSTRE60S1Q320100129 (accessed July 15, 2010).

Ilan, A.M. and D. Ilan. 1996. *You Know You're Drinking Too Much Coffee When…* Holbrook, MA: Adams Media.

Infante, S., M.L. Baeza, M. Calvo, M. De Barrio, M. Rubio, and T. Herrero. 2003. Anaphylaxis Due to Caffeine. *AllergyNet* 58:681–682.

IPNI (International Plant Nutrition Institute). 2009. *Sources of K Fertilizer.* Norcrosse, GA: International Plant Nutrition Institute.

Jaffee, D. 2007. *Brewing Justice: Fair Trade Coffee, Sustainability, and Survival.* Berkeley: University of California Press.

James, P.E. 1932. The Coffee Lands of Southeastern Brazil. *Geographical Review* 22(2):225–244.

Jamieson, R.W. 2001. The Essence of Commodification: Caffeine Dependencies in the Early Modern World. *Journal of Social History* 35(2):269–294.

Jessop, B. 2002. Liberalism, Neoliberalism, and Urban Governance. In *Spaces of Neoliberalism: Urban Restructuring in North America and Western Europe*, ed. N. Brenner and N. Theodore, 105–125. Malden, MA: Wiley-Blackwell.

Jiménez, M.F. 1995a. At the Banquet of Civilization: The Limits of Planter Hegemony in Early Twentieth-Century Colombia. In *Coffee, Society, and Power in Latin America*, ed. W. Roseberry, L. Gudmundson, and M. Samper Kutschbach, 262–293. Baltimore, MD: Johns Hopkins University Press.

Jiménez, M.F. 1995b. "From Plantation to Cup": Coffee and Capitalism in the United States, 1803–1930. In *Coffee, Society and Power in Latin America*, ed. W. Roseberry, L. Gudmundson, and M. Samper Kutschback, 38–64. Baltimore, MD: Johns Hopkins University Press.

Justaboutcoffee.com. 2007. *Coffee Facts.* Online: www.justaboutcoffee.com/index.php?file=facts (accessed July 18, 2010).

Katz, H. 2006. Gramsci, Hegemony, and Global Civil Society Networks. *Voluntas* 17:332–347.

Kurian, R. 2003. Labor, Race and Gender on the Coffee Plantations in Ceylon (Sri Lanka), 1834–1880. In *The Global Coffee Economy in Africa, Asia, and Latin America, 1500–1989*, ed. W.G. Clarence-Smith and S. Topik, 173–190. Cambridge: Cambridge University Press.

Kurlansky, M. 1997. *Cod: A Biography of the Fish That Changed the World.* New York: Walker.

Lafer, C. 2000. Brazilian International Identity and Foreign Policy: Past, Present, and Future. *Daedalus* 129(2):207–238.

Lamarine, R.J. 1998. Caffeine as an Ergogenic Aid. In *Caffeine*, ed. G.A. Spiller, 233–250. Boca Raton, FL: CRC Press.

Lévi-Strauss, C. 1983. *The Raw and the Cooked: Mythologiques Vol. I.* Chicago: University of Chicago Press.

Lévi-Strauss, C. 2008. The Culinary Triangle. In *Food and Culture: A Reader*, 2nd edn, ed. C. Counihan and P. Van Esterik, 36–43. New York: Routledge.

Lopez-Garcia, E., R.M. van Dam, T.Y. Li, F. Rodriguez-Artalejo, and F.B. Hu. 2008. The Relationship of Coffee Consumption with Mortality. *Annals of Internal Medicine* 148:904–914.

Love, R. 1999. Coffee Crunch. *Review of African Political Economy* 26(82):503–508.

Lundsberg, L.S. 1998. Caffeine Consumption. In *Caffeine*, ed. G.A. Spiller, 199–224. Boca Raton, FL: CRC Press.

McCreery, D. 1986. "An Odious Feudalism": Mandamiento Labor and Commercial Agriculture in Guatemala, 1858–1920. *Latin American Perspectives* 13(1):99–117.

McCreery, D. 1995. Wage Labor, Free Labor, and Vagrancy Laws: The Transition to Capitalism in Guatemala. In *Coffee, Society, and Power in Latin America*, ed. W. Roseberry, L. Gudmundson, and M. Samper Kutschbach, 206–231. Baltimore, MD: Johns Hopkins University Press.

MacVean, C.M., J.C. Schuster, and E.B. Cano. 2001. Adaptive Radiation in the Tropics: Entomology at the Universidad del Valle de Guatemala. *American Entomologist* 47:138–144.

Martínez-Torres, M.E. 2006. *Organic Coffee: Sustainable Development by Mayan Farmers*. Athens: University of Ohio Press.

Marx, K. 1978. *Capital*, Volume One. In *The Marx–Engels Reader*, ed. R.C. Tucker, 294–439. New York: W.W. Norton.

Milgram, S. 1967. The Small World Problem. *Psychology Today* 2:60–67.

Miller, J.W., J. Lyons, P. Beckett, I. Johnson, and G. Hitt. 2008. Global Trade Talks Fail as New Giants Flex Muscle. *Wall Street Journal*, Eastern Edition, July 30, 252:A1, A12.

Mintel Oxygen. 2009. *America's Changing Drinking Habits—US—February 2009*. London: Mintel International Group Limited.

Mintz, S.W. 1986. *Sweetness and Power: The Place of Sugar in Modern History*. New York: Penguin Books.

Mintz, S.W. 1996. *Tasting Food, Tasting Freedom: Excursions into Eating, Culture and the Past*. Boston: Beacon Press.

Mintz, S.W. 2002. Food and Eating: Some Persistent Questions. In *Food Nations: Selling Taste in Consumer Societies*, ed. W. Belasco and P. Scranton, 24–32. New York: Routledge.

Mintz, S.W. and C.M. Du Bois. 2002. The Anthropology of Food and Eating. *Annual Review of Anthropology* 31:99–119.

Moguel, P. and V.M. Toledo. 1999. Biodiversity Conservation in Traditional Coffee Systems of Mexico. *Conservation Biology* 13:11–21.

Nawrot, P., S. Jordan, J. Eastwood, J. Rotstein, A. Hugenholtz, and M. Feeley. 2003. Effects of Caffeine on Human Health. *Food Additives & Contaminants: Part A: Chemistry, Analysis, Control, Exposure & Risk Assessment* 20:1–30.

Nehlig, A. and G. Debry. 1994. Caffeine and Sports Activity: A Review. *International Journal of Sports Medicine* 15(5):215–233.

Nigh, R. 1997. Organic Agriculture and Globalization: A Maya Associative Corporation in Chiapas, Mexico. *Human Organization* 56:427–436.

North, D.C. (1990) *Institutions, Institutional Change and Economic Performance*. New York: Cambridge University Press.

O'Grady, E. 2008. *Twitter To Go: One Houston Coffee Shop Makes Its Mark*. Online: http://pistachioconsulting.com/twitter-to-go (accessed July 18, 2010).

Ortiz, S. 1999. *Harvesting Coffee, Bargaining Wages: Rural Labor Markets in Colombia, 1975–1990*. Ann Arbor: University of Michigan Press.

Osorio, N. 2002. *The Global Coffee Crisis: A Threat to Sustainable Development*. London: International Coffee Organization.

Osorio, N. 2003. *Impact of the Coffee Crises on Poverty in Producing Countries*. London: International Coffee Organization. Online: www.ico.org/documents/icc89-5r1e.pdf (accessed January 8, 2010).

Osorio, N. 2005. *Action to Avoid Future Coffee Price Crises*. London: International Coffee Organization.

Paige, J.M. 1993. Coffee and Power in El Salvador. *Latin American Research Review* 28(3):7–40.

Peckenham, N. and A. Street. 1985. *Honduras: Portrait of a Captive Nation*. New York: Praeger.

Pelucchi, C., A. Tavani, and C. La Vecchia. 2008. Coffee and Alcohol Consumption and Bladder Cancer. *Scandinavian Journal of Urology and Nephrology* 42:37–44.

Pendergrast, M. 1999. *Uncommon Grounds: The History of Coffee and How It Transformed Our World*. New York: Basic Books.

Pendergrast, M. 2000. *For God, Country and Coca-Cola*. New York: Basic Books.

Pereira de Melo, H. 2003. Coffee and Development of the Rio de Janeiro Economy, 1888–1920. In *The Global Coffee Economy in Africa, Asia, and Latin America, 1500–1989*, ed. W.G. Clarence-Smith and S. Topik, 360–384. Cambridge: Cambridge University Press.

Pérez Brignoli, H. 1995. Indians, Communists, and Peasants: The 1932 Rebellion in El Salvador. In *Coffee, Society, and Power in Latin America*, ed. W. Roseberry, L. Gudmundson, and M. Samper Kutschbach, 232–261. Baltimore, MD: Johns Hopkins University Press.

Perfecto, I., R.A. Rice, R. Greenberg, and M.E. van der Voort. 1996. Shade Coffee: A Disappearing Refuge for Biodiversity. *BioScience* 46:598–608.

Piro, S. 1996. *Caffeinated Cartoons*. Bala Cynwyd, PA: Laugh Lines Press.

Plaza Sánchez, J.L. 1998. Organic Coffee Production and the Conservation of Natural Resource in Las Margaritas, Chiapas. In *Timber, Tourists, and Temples*, ed. R.B. Primack, D.B. Bray, H.A. Galleti, and I. Ponciano, 299–315. Washington, DC: Island Press.

Pollan, M. 2008. *In Defense of Food: An Eater's Manifesto*. New York: Penguin.

Pomeranz, K. and S. Topik. 2006. *The World That Trade Created: Society, Culture, and the World Economy*, 2nd edn. Armonk, NY: M.E. Sharpe.

Ponte, S. 2001. Behind the Coffee Crisis. *Economic and Political Weekly* 36(46/47):4410–4417.

Ponte, S. 2002. Brewing a Bitter Cup? Deregulation, Quality and the Re-organization of Coffee Marketing in East Africa. *Journal of Agrarian Change* 2(2):248–272.

Prenosil, J.E., M. Hegglin, T.W. Baumann, P.M. Frischknecht, A.W. Kappeler, P. Brodelius, and D. Haldimann. 1987. Purine Alkaloid Producing Cell Cultures: Fundamental Aspects and Possible Applications in Biotechnology. *Enzyme and Microbial Technology* 9:450–458.

Price, J.M. 1989. What Did Merchants Do? Reflections on British Overseas Trade, 1660–1790. *The Journal of Economic History* 49(2):267–284.

Pritchard, J.C. 1855. *The Natural History of Man: Comprising Inquiries into the Modifying Influence of Physical and Moral Agencies on the Different Tribes of the Human Family*. London: H. Baillière.

Reed, T. 2007. *For the Love of Coffee: 61 Things Every Coffee Lover Knows To Be True*. Naperville, IL: Sourcebooks.

Reichert, T. 2003. *The Erotic History of Advertising*. Amherst, NY: Prometheus.

Reuters. 2009. *Global Coffee Consumption Growth Could Ease*. Online: www.flex-news-food.com/console/PageViewer.aspx?page=24043&amp%3Bstr=coffee (accessed July 15, 2010).

Rice, R.A. and J.R. Ward. 1996. *Coffee, Conservation, and Commerce in the Western Hemisphere: How Individuals and Institutions Can Promote Ecologically Sound Farming and Forest Management in Northern Latin America*. Washington, DC: Smithsonian Migratory Bird Center; New York: Natural Resources Defense Council.

Robinson, E. 1972 [1893]. *The Early English Coffee House, with an Account of the First Use of Coffee*. Christchurch, New Zealand: Dolphin Press.

Roseberry, W. 1991. La Falta De Brazos: Land and Labor in the Coffee Economies of Nineteenth-century Latin America. *Theory and Society* 20:351–381.

Roseberry, W. 1995. Introduction. In *Coffee, Society, and Power in Latin America*, ed. W. Rose-berry, L. Gudmundson, and M. Samper Kutschbach, 1–37. Baltimore, MD: Johns Hop-kins University Press.

Roseberry, W. 1996. The Rise of Yuppie Coffees and the Reimagination of Class in the United States. *American Anthropologist* 98:762–775.

Roseberry, W., L. Gudmundson, and M. Samper Kutschbach, eds. 1995. *Coffee, Society, and Power in Latin America*. Baltimore, MD: Johns Hopkins University Press.

Rouse, C. and J. Hoskins. 2004. Purity, Soul Food, and Sunni Islam: Explorations at the Inter-section of Consumption and Resistance. *Cultural Anthropology* 19:226–249.

Ryan, J.C. and A.T. Durning. 1997. *Stuff: The Secret Lives of Everyday Things*. Seattle, WA: Sight-line Institute.

Saito, M. 2009. Sustainable Coffee Production. In *Coffee: Growing, Processing, Sustainable Pro-duction: A Guidebook for Growers, Processors, Traders, and Researchers*, 2nd rev. edn, ed. J.N. Wintgens, 388–394. Weinheim, Germany: Wiley-VCH.

Schivelbusch, W. 1992. *Tastes of Paradise: A Social History of Spices, Stimulants, and Intoxicants*. Trans. D. Jacobsen. New York: Pantheon Books.

Schultz, E.A. and R.H. Lavenda. 2009. *Cultural Anthropology: A Perspective on the Human Con-dition*. Oxford: Oxford University Press.

Sick, D. 2008. *Farmers of the Golden Bean: Costa Rican Households, Global Coffee, and Fair Trade*, rev. edn. DeKalb: Northern Illinois University Press.

Silvera, S.A.N., M. Jain, G.R. Howe, A. Miller, and T.E. Rohan. 2007. Intake of Coffee and Tea and Risk of Ovarian Cancer: A Prospective Cohort Study. *Nutrition and Cancer* 58(1):22–27.

Smith, B.C. 1994. Food Rioters and the American Revolution. *The William and Mary Quarterly* 51:3–38.

Smith, B.D. and K. Tola. 1998. Caffeine: Effects on Psychological Functioning and Perform-ance. In *Caffeine*, ed. G.A. Spiller, 251–300. Boca Raton, FL: CRC Press.

Smith, J. 2007. The Search for Sustainable Markets: The Promise and Failures of Fair Trade. *Culture & Agriculture* 29(2):89–99.

Smith, S.D. 1996. Accounting for Taste: British Coffee Consumption in Historical Perspec-tive. *Journal of Interdisciplinary History* 27(2):183–214.

Spiller, M.A. 1984. The Chemical Components of Coffee. *Progress in Clinical and Biological Research* 158:91–147.

Stafford, T. 2003. Psychology in the Coffee Shop. *The Psychologist* 16:358–359.

Standage, T. 2005. *A History of the World in 6 Glasses*. New York: Walker & Company.

Stanford, D.D. 2007. Coca-Cola Blak Fizzles. *U.S. Atlanta Journal-Constitution*, August 31, 1G.

Starbucks Coffee Company. 2010a. *Company Profile*. Online: http://assets.starbucks.com/assets/company-profile-feb10.pdf (accessed July 18, 2010).

Starbucks Coffee Company. 2010b. *Our Heritage*. Online: www.starbucks.com/about-us/our-heritage (accessed July 17, 2010).

Steevens, J., L.J. Schouten, B.A.J. Verhage, R.A. Goldbohm, and P.A. van den Brandt. 2007. Tea and Coffee Drinking and Ovarian Cancer Risk: Results from the Netherlands Cohort Study and a Meta-Analysis. *British Journal of Cancer* 97:1291–1294.

Stensvold, I., A. Tverdal, and O.P. Foss. 1989. The Effect of Coffee on Blood Lipids and Blood Pressure. Results from a Norwegian Cross-Sectional Study, Men and Women, 40–42 Years. *Journal of Clinical Epidemiology* 42(9):877–884.

Stolke, V. 1995. The Labors of Coffee in Latin America: The Hidden Charm of Family Labor and Self-Provisioning. In *Coffee, Society and Power in Latin America*, ed. W. Roseberry, L. Gudmundson, and M. Samper Kutschbach, 65–93. Baltimore, MD: Johns Hopkins Uni-versity Press.

Sweet Maria's Coffee. 2010. *An Updated Visual Guide to the Roast Process*. Online: www.sweet-marias.com/roasting-VisualGuideV2.php (accessed July 20, 2010).

Talbot, J.M. 1997. Where Does Your Coffee Dollar Go?: The Division of Income and Surplus along the Coffee Commodity Chain. *Studies in Comparative International Development* 32(1):56–91.

Talbot, J.M. 2002. Tropical Commodity Chains, Forward Integration Strategies and International Inequality: Coffee, Cocoa, and Tea. *Review of International Political Economy* 9(4):701–734.

Talbot, J.M. 2004. *Grounds for Agreement: The Political Economy of the Coffee Commodity Chain*. Lanham, MD: Rowman & Littlefield.

Tangley, L. 1996. The Case of the Missing Migrants: Are New Methods for Cultivating Coffee in Latin America Bad for Birds? *Science* 274:1299–1300.

Taussig, M. 1978. Peasant Economics and the Development of Capitalist Agriculture in the Cauca Valley, Colombia. *Latin American Perspectives* 5(3):62–91.

Tea & Coffee Trade Journal. 2004. Majority of U.S. Coffeehouses Independent. *Tea & Coffee Trade Journal* 178(4). Online: www.teaandcoffee.net/0404/world.htm (accessed July 26, 2010).

Tea & Coffee Trade Journal. 2007. National Coffee Drinking Trends for 2007. *Tea and Coffee Trade Journal* 179(5):130.

Ten Thousand Villages. 2009. *Our History: Roots of a Global Movement*. Online: www.tenthousandvillages.com/php/contact/index.php (accessed August 28, 2009).

Thomas, R.D. 1995. *Coffee: The Bean of My Existence*. New York: Henry Holt.

Tomlinson, John. 1999. *Globalization and Culture*. Chicago: University of Chicago Press.

Topik, S. 1999. Where Is the Coffee? Coffee and Brazilian Identity. *Luso-Brazilian Review* 36(2):87–92.

Topik, S. 2003. The Integration of the World Coffee Market. In *The Global Coffee Economy in Africa, Asia, and Latin America, 1500–1989*, ed. W.G. Clarence-Smith and S. Topik, 21–49. Cambridge: Cambridge University Press.

Topik, S.C. and W.G. Clarence-Smith, eds. 2003. *The Global Coffee Economy in Africa, Asia, and Latin America, 1500–1989*. Cambridge: Cambridge University Press.

Toye, J. and R. Toye. 2003. The Origins and Interpretation of the Prebisch-Singer Thesis. *History of Political Economy* 35(3):437–467.

Tucker, C.M. 2008. *Changing Forests: Collective Action, Common Property and Coffee in Honduras*. Dordrecht: Springer.

Tucker, C.M., H. Eakin, and E. Castellanos. 2010. Perceptions of Risk and Adaptations: Coffee Producers, Market Shocks and Extreme Weather in Central America and Mexico. *Global Environmental Change* 20:23–32.

Tufts University. 2008. Special Report: Brewing up Health Benefits for Coffee. *Tufts University Health and Nutrition Letter* 4–5.

UCPA (Universal Crop Protection Alliance). 2010. *Thiodan Emulsifiable Concentrate*. Online: www.cdms.net/LabelsMsds/LMDefault.aspx?pd=6328 (accessed July 25, 2010).

Ukers, W.H. 1935. *All about Coffee*. New York: The Tea & Coffee Trade Journal Company.

van Dam, R.M. 2008. Coffee Consumption and Risk of Type 2 Diabetes, Cardiovascular Diseases, and Cancer. *Applied Physiology, Nutrition and Metabolism* 33:1269–1283.

Vandermeer, J. and I. Perfecto. 2005. *Breakfast of Biodiversity: The Political Ecology of Rainforest Destruction*, 2nd edn. Oakland, CA: Food First Books.

Varangis, P., P. Siegel, D. Giovannucci, and B. Lewin. 2003. *Dealing with the Coffee Crisis in Central America: Impacts and Strategies*. Policy Research Working Paper 2993. Washington, DC: World Bank.

Wallerstein, I. 1980. *The Modern World System 1: Capitalist Agriculture and the Origins of the European World-Economy in the Sixteenth Century*. New York: Academic Press.

Waridel, L. 2002. *Coffee with Pleasure: Just Java and World Trade.* New York: Black Rose Books.

Weinberg, B.A. and B.K. Bealer. 2002. *The World of Caffeine: The Science and Culture of the World's Most Popular Drug.* New York: Routledge.

Weiner, M. 2002. Consumer Culture and Participatory Democracy: The Story of Coca-Cola during World War II. In *Food in the USA: A Reader,* ed. C.M. Counihan, 123–142. New York: Routledge.

Wentz, L. and D. Mussey. 2006. Coke to Begin Blak Launch in France. *Advertising Age* 77:23.

Weusten-Van der Wouw, M.P.M.E., M.B. Katan, R. Viani, A.C. Huggett, R. Liardon, P.G. Lund-Larsen, D.S. Thelle, I. Ahola, A. Aro, S. Meyboom, and A.C. Beynen. 1994. Identity of the Cholesterol-Raising Factor from Boiled Coffee and Its Effects on Liver Function Enzymes. *Journal of Lipid Research* 35:721–733.

Wheeler, S. 2005. *How to Be Happy (Too Much Coffee Man).* Milwaukie, OR: Dark Horse.

Wild, A. 2004. *Coffee: A Dark History.* New York: W.W. Norton.

Williams, R.G. 1994. *States and Social Evolution: Coffee and the Rise of National Governments in Central America.* Chapel Hill: University of North Carolina Press.

Winick, M. 1998. Caffeine and Reproduction. In *Caffeine,* ed. G.A. Spiller, 357–362. Boca Raton, FL: CRC Press.

Wintgens, J.N. and A. Zamarripa Colmenero. 2009. Coffee Propagation. In *Coffee: Growing, Processing, Sustainable Production: A Guidebook for Growers, Processors, Traders and Researchers,* 2nd rev. edn, ed. J.N. Wintgens, 91–140. Weinheim, Germany: Wiley-VCH Verlag.

Winzeler, R.L. 2008. *Anthropology and Religion: What We Know, Think and Question.* Lanham, MD: Rowman & Littlefield.

Wolf, E.R. 1982. *Europe and the People without History.* Berkeley: University of California Press.

Worsley, P. 1990. Models of the Modern World-System. *Theory, Culture & Society* 7(2):83–95.

Zuckerman, L. 1998. *The Potato: How the Humble Spud Rescued the Western World.* Boston: Faber & Faber.

INDEX

Page numbers in *italics* denote tables, those in **bold** denote figures.